# ENDORSEMENTS

I just read *Intervention Prayers* and can truthfully say this book is unlike any I've ever read. It is equipping, powerful, life-transforming, written by one who needed the intervening power of God and received it. The book says that "If someone you love is fighting for their life, trapped in addiction, or deceived by destructive forces, this book is for you." I couldn't agree more. Believe me when I tell you this book will help anyone. *I am honored* that I was asked to write an endorsement for this powerful book!

**Rick Renner**
Rick Renner Ministries
Moscow, Russia

For every loving person who has ever prayed the prayer of desperation on behalf of a family member or friend, here at last is a book that will guide you out of desperation into powerful, effective prayer. When you realize God is on your side, your faith will reach new levels.

Michelle has found the secrets of prayer that work in her own life and for her family. Let her knowledge of God's love and compassion spill over onto you, encourage you, and enable you to stand in the gap for your loved ones.

**Annette Capps**
Capps Ministries
Tulsa, Oklahoma

There have been many books written on prayer, and each has unique value. However, rarely does a book come along that is written from the perspective of a recipient of life-changing intervention prayer.

Michelle's book is one of these. She writes from firsthand experience as someone whose life was saved by persistent, effective, and powerful prayer!

Each chapter not only gives Bible examples and other testimonies of how prayer intervened in an otherwise hopeless situation but also gives the reader words to pray and the Word to build faith.

Written as a devotional, this book can become a first response "go-to" on a daily basis. You will be equipped and built up to pray not only fervently but effectively for miraculous results.

**Patsy Cameneti**
Rhema Family Church
Brisbane, Australia

# INTERVENTION
# PRAYERS

Harrison House

Shippensburg, PA

# INTERVENTION
# PRAYERS

## POWERFUL PRAYERS TO
## RESCUE & RESTORE
## YOUR FAMILY

# MICHELLE STEELE

# DEDICATION

I dedicate this book to all of those who are holding the lives of their loved ones up before God, standing in faith for their lives to be free from destruction, and believing to see the goodness of the Lord in the land of the living. May Psalm 22:5 (AMP) be established in your lives:

*They cried out to You and were delivered; they trusted in You and were not disappointed or ashamed.*

# CONTENTS

## WEEK THREE

## WEEK FOUR

# "911...WHAT'S YOUR EMERGENCY?"

The frantic family member hears the voice of the 911 operator and knows they have connected with their lifeline. Relief rushes in, and the fear of losing their loved one is replaced with hope. Within minutes, lifesaving resources are dispatched. Help is on its way!

If someone you love is fighting for their life, trapped in addiction, or deceived by destructive forces, this book is for you! This book, founded on God's Word, will help you make the call to Heaven's 911 Call Center and relay the proper information to have God's lifesaving resources dispatched to your loved one's location.

Your 911 call is vital to the rescue of your loved one. The 911 operator sends the help, but there may be some things you need to do until help arrives. In the same way, there are things the Lord will have you pray that will open the way for Him to work. He may have you pray for laborers to be sent across the path of your loved one. The Lord may prompt you to pray for protection or plead the blood of Jesus. So stay on the line!

Many people trapped in a destructive lifestyle have lost the power to change their situation. Perhaps they began using drugs or alcohol in high school or college because it was how they "partied" on the weekends. But after years of submitting themselves to the control of alcohol or drugs, they are unable to stop. They've lost control! Now, they need someone who has a covenant with God to intercede for them.

If you feel desperate whenever you talk to God about your loved one, I have prepared this book just for you! Seeing the people you love struggle with an addiction or destructive lifestyle can be frustrating and tormenting. You need to know how to stand and release your faith regardless of what you see playing out in their lives.

I want to help you stand strong in the ability that God provides. Isaiah 40:31 says, "*But those who wait on the Lord shall renew their strength; they shall mount up with wings like eagles, they shall run and not be weary, they shall walk and not faint.*" As you trust in Him, the Lord will renew your strength! When the Lord says that you will "mount up with wings like eagles," it brings to my mind the eagle climbing in altitude above the storm. See yourself lifted above the situation, clearly seeing how to help your loved one.

In the pages of this book, you will find answers. You will learn how to resist and how to use your faith and authority as spiritual weapons. With four weeks of faith, divided into daily doses of God's Word, you will find direction and focus to pray with purpose. Each week begins with a testimony to jumpstart your faith in God's willingness to save, followed by daily teaching with vital keys to unlocking the lifesaving assistance your loved one needs.

The prayers are packed with God's Word and designed to show you how to structure your petitions in line with God's will. Specific verses are strategically placed at the end of each daily concept so you can turn your attention away from the circumstantial evidence and focus on the proof of God's faithfulness. Let the prayers found in this book help you to jump-start your conversation and petitions to God. In other words, let these prayers get you started, but continue on your own, finding verses that the Holy Spirit leads you to use and dealing with specific situations that your loved one is facing.

This is not the type of book you read once and set it on the shelf. When you finish the book, after applying the concepts and releasing your faith in prayer, you will want to start over. As you do, you will gain practice with the concepts you have learned. You will strengthen the foundation that was established with the first read-through.

Please seek God for His plan as you go through this book because God has a specific plan to set your loved ones free that will require spiritual and natural resources. You may be facing life-threatening situations with your family members. God may lead you to find help in a treatment center, counseling services, or a support group. God can use all these things to help you win this battle.

As you pray your intervention prayers, visualize God's first responders loading their equipment, climbing into their emergency vehicles, and setting their GPS with the coordinates of your loved one. Stay on the line, follow Heaven's instructions, and be assured that help is on the way!

# WEEK ONE

## INTERVENTION STORY:
# A PRODUCT OF PRAYER

I never told my parents about the sexual abuse I had suffered at the hands of the junior high coach or by the caretaker of the barn where my horse had been stabled. They thought it was teenage rebellion, but it was more dangerous than that. At the age of fifteen, I ran away from home. My family didn't understand the inner turmoil I suffered or the destruction breeding in my heart.

Many decisions made in the darkness moved me onto the path of a rebellious, drug-addicted prostitute. It didn't happen overnight, but I found myself on a dead-end street of self-hatred. I continued on a roller coaster of addiction for years, piercing my veins with hypodermic needles to chase a high that was never enough. Numerous encounters with the police, arrests, and drug charges accumulated until I was arrested for three counts of attempted armed robbery.

Still, it wasn't enough to make me change my direction. After my partner-in-crime died of a drug overdose, my life spiraled out of control. In the back of a bar in the projects of East Nashville, I inserted the needle in my vein and emptied the abundant dose of cocaine into my arm. Instead of the anticipated high, I met death. My heart stopped, and I found myself standing in front of a skull. Hands of darkness began to reach for me, trying to pull me into hell. I ran back to my body and continued running. I ran out of the bar and down the street before I realized I was back in my body. (For my complete testimony, read *Escaping Hell, A True Story: God's Miraculous Power to Restore a Life Bent on Destruction.*)

I went to church that evening. I began looking for God, wanting to change my ways and needing His help. Thankfully, God had troops on the ground, people who would reach out and help a complex case like mine. I accepted Jesus as Lord, connected to a local church, and began to learn about God, His Word, and His ways. The Lord rebuilt my life, restored relationships, and placed me in the ministry.

At first, I wondered what made the difference in my outcome. As I learned about the authority a believer has in prayer, I saw the answer to my question. My family explained how they had asked the Lord to save me. My children made special requests in Sunday school for God to turn my life around. Because people in my family had opened the door to God's power, giving Him legal access to intervene, the Lord could show me His mercy and send His laborers across my path.

When a person calls 911, they invite the help that is available and on standby. With that call, help is accessed and activated. That is what happened when my children asked their Sunday school teacher to agree in prayer. They called 911 and sent God's help to me. When my grandma and mom prayed, asking God to set me free, they connected to God's helpline. Each time, the Lord sent power to my location. I had to accept His help and power, but without their calls, the power would not have had legal access to me.

The prayers of my loved ones became a legal invitation that sent Jesus and His help to my location. Yet, I know from their testimonies it was a struggle to maintain their faith. They didn't know how to resist what was happening to me or to stand in a place of authority to petition on my behalf. They knew God was my only hope, but they weren't sure how to get Him to help me.

In telling the story of my life and how God rescued me, I have met many people with family members living in addiction and crime. Their faces reveal the anguish and anxiety that is abundantly in their hearts. As they describe the details of how desperate the situation is in the lives of their loved ones, they plead with me to pray for their family. My heart goes out to each of them because I know their prayers are weighed down with hopelessness instead of faith and expectation of deliverance.

# DAY 1

# PURSUE, OVERTAKE, AND RECOVER ALL!

The Bible speaks of a man named David who called for God's intervention when his family was captured. His situation offered no hope or answer. By all appearances, it was too late. The Amalekites had burned the city of Ziklag to the ground and taken all the people captive—even the families of David and his soldiers.

## 1 SAMUEL 30:1-5

*Now it happened, when David and his men came to Ziklag, on the third day, that the Amalekites had invaded the South and Ziklag, attacked Ziklag and burned it with fire, and had taken captive the women and those who were there, from small to great; they did not kill anyone, but carried them away and went their way.*

*So David and his men came to the city, and there it was, burned with fire; and their wives, their sons, and their daughters had been taken captive. Then David and the people who were with him lifted up their voices and wept, until they had no more power to weep. And David's two wives, Ahinoam the Jezreelitess, and Abigail the widow of Nabal the Carmelite, had been taken captive.*

When David and his men returned home and discovered their families were gone, the soldiers were so grief-stricken that they talked about killing David. What a strange way to respond! But their grief was so strong they wanted to release it by hurting someone.

You may have grief and sorrow caused by the situations of your loved ones. But grief, sorrow, or anger won't help you in this intervention. You can't allow the feeling of loss to control you. Instead, you must stay in a place where faith can operate.

Seek the Lord and find out how He wants you to respond to the situation. That's what David did. He inquired of the Lord. He said, "Lord, do You want me to pursue them?"

The Lord said, "Pursue and overtake them. You will recover all."

### 1 SAMUEL 30:6-8

*Now David was greatly distressed, for the people spoke of stoning him, because the soul of all the people was grieved, every man for his sons and his daughters. But David strengthened himself in the Lord his God.*

*Then David said to Abiathar the priest, Ahimelech's son, "Please bring the ephod here to me." And Abiathar brought the ephod to David. So David inquired of the Lord, saying, "Shall I pursue this troop? Shall I overtake them?"*

*And He answered him, "Pursue, for you shall surely overtake them and without fail recover all."*

When David received the instruction from the Lord, he responded spiritually and put away his grief. Even if you receive reports telling you that nothing is going right and things are getting worse, you don't have to let the report dictate your response. You are not moved by situations. You are the situation mover! You are not moved by the mountain. The mountain is moved by you!

If David had not turned to the Lord, his family would have been lost. Instead, David connected to the power of God and became a tool that the Lord could use to rescue his family.

David's intervention brought the power of God into the situation and turned it around. David accessed a supernatural strength to rescue and restore his family and the families of all his soldiers. David recovered all!

You can use your faith and change the situation. You can resist the destruction raging in your loved ones' lives with the Word of God and your covenant with Him. You can apply the life of God to their situations and the blood of Jesus over their paths. When you use these spiritual instruments, you give God an opportunity to get involved in their lives.

Taking authority in the name of Jesus gives God the liberty to operate in that situation. If you don't, who will? That is what you must remember. Who else in your family is hearing instructions from the Lord? You are!

## FIRST RESPONDERS MUST STAY CALM

If you call 911 with an emergency, the 911 operator will help you stay calm and focused. They ask questions to assess the situation and determine what needs to be done first. Then, they give instructions on how to administer help to the victim.

You are "on the phone" with God when you pray. He wants you to remain calm and assess the situation from a spiritual perspective. Trust in the Lord because help is on the way. Intervention is coming! While waiting for the ambulance, stay on the phone and receive His instructions because spiritual, life-saving treatment needs to be administered.

The love you have for this person and the relationship you have with them provide spiritual access. You have a God-given right to set up an intervention and the authority to pray for transformation. But you must maintain your determination to hold on until the going on comes on! This is a time to put patience to work and stand on the covenant you have with God.

My family prayed for me while I was walking the streets of Nashville, Tennessee, prostituting my body to get my next fix. So many people thought they knew how my life would end, but love rewrote my story!

It is not going to end the way the situation has been telling you it is going to end. You are going to take God's Word and rewrite this story. God's love will reach your loved one through the vehicle of your prayers. Stay on the line because help is on the way!

## YOUR INTERVENTION PRAYER

Father God, I am calling for Your intervention in Jesus' name. I am coming to You because someone I love needs Your help. *(Insert your loved one's name)* has been held in bondage to something destroying his/her life. Only You have the power to set them free from this destruction. I come before Your throne to set up a divine intervention in their life.

Heavenly Father, You are fully aware of everything in this situation. You know even the things that are done in secret. You know the tears they have cried. You know the lies the enemy has used to deceive them. Father, You know what it will take to reach them with Your Word and free them from the enemy's hold. I trust in Your help.

You instruct me in Your Word to ask, so I am asking for an intervention. I call on the name of my Savior, Jesus Christ, for deliverance in this situation to stop the destruction and release *(insert your loved one's name)* from all bondage. I take my place in Christ to administer the life-saving prayers and exercise authority over the adversary in their lives.

I open my heart to the leading of the Holy Spirit. I want to be an instrument in Your hands to administer life-saving treatment. I want to take the spiritual action to enforce my covenant and see Your salvation manifest in *(insert your loved one's name)*'s life.

I will not panic. Instead, I will trust You. I ask You to cover *(insert your loved one's name)* with Your mercy and protection. Guard him/her against the dangers of the lifestyle he/she is living. I ask for angels to be commissioned to guard him/her against all tragedy.

I speak life to *(insert your loved one's name)* and command thoughts of death, suicide, and self-harm to stop. Every stronghold of death, be broken in the name of Jesus! Let the peace of God surround his/her heart and mind. Let there be hope where the enemy has tried to plant hopelessness. I command a crop failure on the seeds of death the devil has sown.

Father, Your Word declares if I believe on the Lord Jesus Christ, I will be saved, and my family too. I stand on that promise! I claim the salvation of *(insert your loved one's name)*. I believe I will see the goodness of God in *(insert your loved one's name)*'s life.

# BUILD YOUR FAITH

## PSALM 5:11

*But let all those rejoice who put their trust in You; let them ever shout for joy, because You defend them; let those also who love Your name be joyful in You.*

## PSALM 9:10

*And those who know Your name will put their trust in You; for You, Lord, have not forsaken those who seek You.*

## PSALM 40:16 (AMPC)

*Let all those that seek and require You rejoice and be glad in You; let such as love Your salvation say continually, The Lord be magnified!*

## PSALM 46:1 (AMPC)

*God is our Refuge and Strength [mighty and impenetrable to temptation], a very present and well-proved help in trouble.*

# ORGANIZE GOD'S RESCUE

The runner appeared above the horizon, struggling to catch his breath, desperate to deliver his message. Abram's nephew, Lot, and his family were taken captive! The battle had been fierce, but the enemy prevailed. The enemy had taken Lot, his family, and all the people of the city.

## GENESIS 14:8-14

*And the king of Sodom, the king of Gomorrah, the king of Admah, the king of Zeboiim, and the king of Bela (that is, Zoar) went out and joined together in battle in the Valley of Siddim against Chedorlaomer king of Elam, Tidal king of nations, Amraphel king of Shinar, and Arioch king of Ellasar—four kings against five. Now the Valley of Siddim was full of asphalt pits; and the kings of Sodom and Gomorrah fled; some fell there, and the remainder fled to the mountains. Then they took all the goods of Sodom and Gomorrah, and all their provisions, and went their way. They also took Lot, Abram's brother's son who dwelt in Sodom, and his goods, and departed.*

*Then one who had escaped came and told Abram the Hebrew, for he dwelt by the terebinth trees of Mamre the Amorite, brother of Eshcol and brother of Aner; and they were allies with Abram. Now when Abram heard that his brother was taken captive, he armed his three hundred and eighteen trained servants who were born in his own house, and went in pursuit as far as Dan.*

What would Abram do? What *could* he do? The enemy forces had defeated five armies of trained soldiers! How would Abram be able to rescue Lot and his family? Maybe you have asked yourself a similar question. *What can I do? How can I help them?*

Lot had no power to free himself. He was helpless in this battle, having no weapons, power, or authority. That is the case with some of our loved ones. We see them in bondage to addiction or trapped in a destructive lifestyle, and we think they can stop when they get ready, not realizing the enemy's supernatural hold over their lives. They don't have the power to free themselves from the spiritual bondage that comes with that addiction or deception.

Also, Lot put himself in this dangerous position by choosing to live in Sodom. Your loved one may have chosen to hang out with the wrong sort of people, to start drinking, to put a needle in their arm, or to start smoking a crack pipe. Maybe they have submitted to alcohol or drugs so often that it has taken a position of dominion. When I was an addict, it didn't happen overnight, but each time I gave myself to that drug, it controlled me more and more. Eventually, addiction took the lordship of my life. The time came when it was directing the course of my life.

Blaming your loved one won't help. Yes, they made the mess. They chose it. But you must take your covenant with God and make the 911 call. Abram didn't say, "Lot is getting what he deserves. He made this bed. Let him lie in it." No! Abram didn't blame Lot.

Abram didn't hesitate or withdraw from the situation because it looked impossible, nor did he question God's willingness to save his nephew. On the contrary, Abram knew he had to help and trusted that God was on his side. Abram gathered the 318 men who worked in his fields and went to free Lot and the others from their captivity.

In the same way, you must have confidence in God's willingness to save. Regardless of the poor decisions your loved ones have made to cause their despair, God will help you reach them. Despite the laws they've broken, the things they've done to hurt themselves, or whatever addictions they may have, God is full of mercy and compassion. He sent Jesus to seek and save the lost. He will help us reach them!

Without an intervention of God's power, your loved one may waste away in captivity. But, glory to God, you are in the process of intervention.

## GENESIS 14:15-17

*He divided his forces against them by night, and he and his servants attacked them and pursued them as far as Hobah, which is north of Damascus. So he brought back all the goods, and also brought back his brother Lot and his goods, as well as the women and the people.*

*And the king of Sodom went out to meet him at the Valley of Shaveh (that is, the King's Valley), after his return from the defeat of Chedorlaomer and the kings who were with him.*

With 318 men, Abram accomplished what the five kingdoms' armies failed to do. It wasn't the skill of servants in the battle that won the victory because they were ranch hands—not soldiers. What made the difference? Abram was in covenant with God and provided an open door for the Lord to rescue Lot and all those who were taken captive by the enemy.

Lot may have been lost forever if Abram had not intervened. But God was with Abram, and God is with you!

## YOUR INTERVENTION PRAYER

God, I approach Your holy throne in the name of my Lord Jesus Christ. I am thankful for the covenant You have made for my family and me. You said that You would be with me in trouble (Ps. 91:15). I stand on that promise and give You praise.

Psalm 86:7 declares, *"In the day of my trouble I will call upon You, for You will answer me."* I walk in the fullness of that provision, Lord. I call out in the name of Jesus for the supernatural rescue of *(insert your loved one's name).* By my faith in Your covenant, I receive the complete freedom of *(insert your loved one's name).*

As a representative of Jesus Christ, I speak to the enemy forces holding *(insert your loved one's name)* in captivity. I command you to release your hold on him/her completely. Let every lie that has blinded his/her mind from the truth of the gospel of Jesus Christ be brought into the light. Deception, be exposed! Unbelief, be broken!

I apply the blood of Jesus to cover *(insert your loved one's name).* No weapon formed against them will be able to prosper. No evil will befall them. Nothing shall by any means hurt them. May the blood of Jesus protect them from all the attempts of Satan to destroy them. I draw the bloodline around their lives like a property line. Death and injury are not permitted in this life! They are kept by the power of God.

By faith, I administer the mercy of God to *(insert your loved one's name)*'s situation. Father, even in situations caused by their own actions and rebellion, I call for mercy to prevail. Let the love of God be made known to them in a very real way.

Now, I lift my hands to heaven and rejoice. Victory is ours. *(Insert your loved one's name)* belongs to the kingdom of Jesus Christ.

# BUILD YOUR FAITH

## ISAIAH 49:25 (NLT)

*But the Lord says, "The captives of warriors will be released, and the plunder of tyrants will be retrieved. For I will fight those who fight you, and **I will save your children**."*

## 1 JOHN 5:14-15

*Now this is the confidence that we have in Him, that if we ask anything according to His will, He hears us. And if we know that He hears us, whatever we ask, we know that we have the petitions that we have asked of Him.*

## DEUTERONOMY 7:9

*Therefore know that the Lord your God, He is God, the faithful God who keeps covenant and mercy for a thousand generations with those who love Him and keep His commandments.*

## PSALM 22:4

*Our fathers trusted in You; they trusted, and You delivered them.*

# PUT INTERVENTION IN GEAR

Many people think prayer is powerful regardless of how it is prayed. They say, "As long as I am praying...." But if you start the car and press down on the gas pedal, you haven't started driving. Until you put the transmission in drive, you won't see any progress, and until you put intervention into the gear of faith, you won't see any change.

If you pray what you see, think, or feel, you are praying in neutral. Some people pray in neutral because their emotions negate their faith. They close their eyes and lift their voices to pray, but they connect their mouths to their feelings and rehearse the sadness, anxiety, or fear caused by what they see in the lives of their loved ones. You can spend all your strength spinning your spiritual wheels, and nothing has changed.

Also, if you pray the problem, you are praying in reverse. The danger is that it feels good to release your feelings. You feel better for a few minutes because you have unloaded your emotional baggage. But the feeling is momentary. You have deceived yourself, thinking you have accomplished something spiritual and effective.

Emotional prayers talk about what is happening and how it makes us feel. They make us tired and sad. Spiritual prayers talk about what the Word of God says and are full of thanksgiving to God. Spiritual prayers have a sound of victory and authority, and they make us strong.

One of my favorite examples of an intervention by God is found in the life of the woman of Shunem, who prayed for her son. First, we see that she had prepared a place of honor for Elisha because he was a man of God.

## 2 KINGS 4:9-10

*And she said to her husband, "Look now, I know that this is a holy man of God, who passes by us regularly. Please, let us make a small upper room on the wall; and let us put a bed for him there, and a table and a chair and a lampstand; so it will be, whenever he comes to us, he can turn in there."*

This represents honor for God and His Word. We should prepare a place for the Word in our lives—a place of honor. If you haven't done this yet, do it now. Make the decision to honor the Word of God over the problem. Make time for His Word daily and honor His ways.

The Shunammite woman's honor for God caused the supernatural peace of God to flow to the area of her heart's desire. This peace supernaturally restores broken and empty places. Peace produces a life with nothing missing and nothing broken. She had never had children, but God's peace provided her greatest desire.

## 2 KINGS 4:18-23

*And the child grew. Now it happened one day that he went out to his father, to the reapers. And he said to his father, "My head, my head!"*

*So he said to a servant, "Carry him to his mother." When he had taken him and brought him to his mother, he sat on her knees till noon, and then died. And she went up and laid him on the*

*bed of the man of God, shut the door upon him, and went out. Then she called to her husband, and said, "Please send me one of the young men and one of the donkeys, that I may run to the man of God and come back."*

*So he said, "Why are you going to him today? It is neither the New Moon nor the Sabbath."*

*And she said, "It is well."*

What a response! She said, "It is well." In the original language, it is the word *shalom*, which means "wholeness, completeness, nothing is missing, and nothing is broken." The Shunammite woman sought God's help with faith that He would restore her son. Her persistence provided an avenue through which God's power could restore life to her son.

Most importantly, the woman of Shunem spoke from the covenant and not her emotions. When her husband asked her why she was going to see the prophet, the woman said, *"It is well."* She wasn't responding in the light of how she felt. She was a woman focused on an intervention. She responded in *faith!*

In Hebrew, the definition of the word *shalom* includes the concept of wholeness. In other words, she was declaring, "I have the peace that comes from being made whole. I have nothing missing and nothing broken in my life." She responded with that declaration whenever she was asked about her well-being.

## 2 KINGS 4:24-26

*Then she saddled a donkey, and said to her servant, "Drive, and go forward; do not slacken the pace for me unless I tell you." And so she departed, and went to the man of God at Mount Carmel.*

*So it was, when the man of God saw her afar off, that he said to his servant Gehazi, "Look, the Shunammite woman! Please run now to meet her, and say to her, 'Is it well with you? Is it well with your husband? Is it well with the child?'"*

*And she answered, "It is well."*

Her son's present condition wasn't the focus of her activity. Her declaration was not based on what she could see or what she felt. The man of God recognized that she was dealing with something serious and said, *"Let her alone; for her soul is in deep distress."* (2 Kings 4:27) Her emotions were real, but she didn't permit them to have control over the way she responded to the problem.

## 2 KINGS 4:32-37

*When Elisha came into the house, there was the child, lying dead on his bed. He went in therefore, shut the door behind the two of them, and prayed to the Lord. And he went up and lay on the child, and put his mouth on his mouth, his eyes on his eyes, and his hands on his hands; and he stretched himself out on the child, and the flesh of the child became warm. He returned and walked back and forth in the house, and again went up and stretched himself out on him; then the child sneezed seven times, and the child opened his eyes. And he called Gehazi and said, "Call this Shunammite woman." So he called her. And when she came in to him, he said, "Pick up your son." So she went in, fell at his feet, and bowed to the ground; then she picked up her son and went out.*

The Shunammite woman engaged her covenant with God and put her intervention in the gear of faith. Her son received complete restoration because she sought God with confidence that He would help. She became an instrument in the hand of God, and we can do the same!

You can approach God on behalf of your loved ones just like this woman of Shunem. You can connect God's life, mercy, and love to their desperate situations and change them! You can release your faith for God's restoration and see His power work on their behalf. She used her covenant with God to connect her family members to God's help, and so will you!

## YOUR INTERVENTION PRAYER

Father God, I approach You in the Name of my Lord Jesus Christ. I ask You to forgive me for any prayers I have brought to You that were out of line with Your Word. I believe that You hear me when I pray and want to answer my prayers. I ask You to teach me to pray Your Word. Lord, show me things from Your truth that I can use when I pray for *(insert your loved one's name)*.

I stand on Your Word and declare, "Great shall be the peace, the condition of nothing missing, and nothing broken of *(insert your loved one's name)*" (Isa. 54:13). *(Insert your loved one's name)* will not be taken from me. He/she will not be separated from me in this life or the life to come. I release my faith for his/her salvation. According to Matthew 13:15 (AMPC), I pray that *(insert your loved one's name)* would see and perceive with their eyes, hear and comprehend with their ears, grasp and understand with their heart so they can turn, and You will save them.

I refuse to talk about how the situation makes me feel. Instead, I come to You rejoicing because Your Word is Truth. You said when I ask, I shall receive. You said when I seek, I will find. You said when I knock, it shall be opened to me. Lord, I ask You to speak to *(insert your loved one's name)* today. Lord, I am seeking You for mercy to be shown to *(insert your loved one's name)* today. Lord, I am knocking on the door to opportunity for *(insert your loved one's name)* to see the light of the gospel.

Heavenly Father, in Jeremiah 23:29 (AMPC), You said that Your Word is like a hammer that breaks in pieces the rock of most stubborn resistance. I take the hammer of Your Word and strike the mind-blinding devices the enemy has placed on *(insert your loved one's name)'s* mind. You draw them out of the dominion of darkness into the kingdom of Your dear Son, in Jesus' name.

I choose to rejoice now, even before I see any changes in this situation. I govern my emotions by exalting Your truth above my facts. I choose to praise Your name and lift my voice. You are my light and my salvation! You are the strength of my life! I will not be afraid (Ps. 27:1).

## BUILD YOUR FAITH

### ISAIAH 54:13 (AMPC)

*And all your [spiritual] children shall be disciples [taught by the Lord and obedient to His will], and great shall be the peace and undisturbed composure of your children.*

## ISAIAH 54:17 (AMPC)

*But no weapon that is formed against you shall prosper, and every tongue that shall rise against you in judgment you shall show to be in the wrong. This [peace, righteousness, security, triumph over opposition] is the heritage of the servants of the Lord [those in whom the ideal Servant of the Lord is reproduced]; this is the righteousness or the vindication which they obtain from Me [this is that which I impart to them as their justification], says the Lord.*

## COLOSSIANS 1:13 (AMPC)

*[The Father] has delivered and drawn us to Himself out of the control and the dominion of darkness and has transferred us into the kingdom of the Son of His love.*

## JEREMIAH 23:29 (AMPC)

*Is not My word like fire [that consumes all that cannot endure the test]? says the Lord, and like a hammer that breaks in pieces the rock [of most stubborn resistance]?*

# TAKE GOD AT HIS WORD

Some of the most remarkable displays of faith were requests for intervention. Perhaps it is connected to the seriousness of the situation or the motivation of love for that person, but we see impressive examples of faith as people ask Jesus to help their loved ones. For example, the centurion came to Jesus asking for the healing of someone who lived in his house.

## MATTHEW 8:5-13

*Now when Jesus had entered Capernaum, a centurion came to Him, pleading with Him, saying, "Lord, my servant is lying at home paralyzed, dreadfully tormented."*

*And Jesus said to him, "I will come and heal him."*

*The centurion answered and said, "Lord, I am not worthy that You should come under my roof. But only speak a word, and my servant will be healed. For I also am a man under authority, having soldiers under me. And I say to this one, 'Go,' and he goes; and to another, 'Come,' and he comes; and to my servant, 'Do this,' and he does it."*

*When Jesus heard it, He marveled, and said to those who followed, "Assuredly, I say to you, I have not found such great faith, not even in Israel! And I say to you that many will come from*

*east and west, and sit down with Abraham, Isaac, and Jacob in the kingdom of heaven. But the sons of the kingdom will be cast out into outer darkness. There will be weeping and gnashing of teeth." Then Jesus said to the centurion, "Go your way; and as you have believed, so let it be done for you." And his servant was healed that same hour.*

He said, "You don't even have to come to my house. Speak the word only, and my servant shall be healed." Jesus marveled and said to those who followed Him, "Truly, I have not found such great faith even in Israel."

The centurion's faith provoked a response from Jesus. The Lord said it was the greatest faith He had encountered in the land. What was so remarkable about the faith of this Roman centurion? Let's look at some of the vital elements of the centurion's great faith that will help us too.

One essential element of his faith is that the centurion took Jesus' words as the final authority to heal his servant. He based it on his own experience as a leader in the Roman army. He explained that his authority to lead and direct his soldiers was activated by his words.

Simply, he told his soldiers what to do, and they did it. The centurion applied this same understanding to the authority of Jesus to heal his servant. He recognized that when Jesus sent His words, the things to which Jesus spoke obeyed His commands. In the same manner, we connect our loved ones to the life-saving power of Jesus Christ as we take Him at His Word.

## MATTHEW 8:13

*Then Jesus said to the centurion, "Go your way; and **as you have believed, so let it be done for you.**" And his servant was healed that same hour.*

Notice the phrase *"as you have believed."* Jesus often indicated that the person's faith was involved in what and how they received. For example, in the case of healing the two blind men who came to Him, Jesus said, *"According to your faith."*

## MATTHEW 9:27-30

*When Jesus departed from there, two blind men followed Him, crying out and saying, "Son of David, have mercy on us!"*

*And when He had come into the house, the blind men came to Him. And Jesus said to them, "**Do you believe** that I am able to do this?"*

*They said to Him, "Yes, Lord."*

*Then He touched their eyes, saying, "**According to your faith** let it be to you." And their eyes were opened.*

In another instance, we find the woman of Canaan who asked Jesus to help her daughter, who was being tormented by a devil. Here is Jesus' response:

## MATTHEW 15:28

*Then Jesus answered and said to her, "O woman, great is your faith! **Let it be to you as you desire.**" And her daughter was healed from that very hour.*

Also, to the woman who had the issue of blood, Jesus said it was her faith that made her whole!

## MARK 5:34

*And He said to her, "Daughter, **your faith has made you well.** Go in peace, and be healed of your affliction."*

So, Jesus said, "According to your faith, let it be as you desire," and, "Your faith has made you whole." Those statements reveal a lot about how much our faith affects the outcome of a situation. Our faith plays a major role in what God can do in our lives and the lives of those we love. That is why Ephesians 3:20 records, *"Now to Him who is able to do exceedingly abundantly above all that we ask or think, according to the power that works in us."* God's power is not limiting us. Our faith, or lack of faith, determines what God can do in our situation.

So, how do we know what the centurion believed? If I asked you, "What do you believe?" you would open your mouth and tell me. Jesus said the mouth speaks what is abundantly in the heart (Matt. 12:34). As we study the words of the centurion, we have evidence of how he believed. The centurion said, *"Speak the word only, and my servant shall be healed."*

As we examine what Jairus said when he asked Jesus to heal his daughter, we will discover what he believed.

## MARK 5:22-24

*And behold, one of the rulers of the synagogue came, Jairus by name. And when he saw Him, he fell at His feet and begged Him earnestly, saying, "My little daughter lies at the point of death. Come **and lay Your hands on her, that she may be**

41

*healed, and **she will live.*** *So Jesus went with him, and a great multitude followed Him and thronged Him.*

The statement that Jairus made is what he believed. Jairus said, *"Lay thy hands on her...and she shall live."* Jesus agreed to accompany Jairus to his home and heal his daughter. Along the way, the woman with an issue of blood was healed. Jesus stopped in the crowd, and while there, people from Jairus' house came with bad news.

## MARK 5:35-36

*While He was still speaking, some came from the ruler of the synagogue's house who said, "Your daughter is dead. Why trouble the Teacher any further?"*

*As soon as Jesus heard the word that was spoken, He said to the ruler of the synagogue, "Do not be afraid; only believe."*

When the situation looked worse, Jesus cautioned Jairus, *"Only believe."* In other words, "Your faith is already in motion. Don't take your faith out of gear but allow it to continue moving toward the end result."

In both examples, these men released their faith through their words, and faith-filled words functioned like electrical wires to conduct God's power into their loved ones' lives. As you build faith in God's willingness to rescue your loved one, you are laying the electrical wires to transmit God's power to them. As you continue to pray the intervention prayers, resisting the influence of the enemy and releasing the light and wisdom of God, you are making a lifesaving connection!

# YOUR INTERVENTION PRAYER

Heavenly Father, You said all things I ask in prayer, believing, I shall receive (Mark 11:24). So, I take You at Your Word. I believe, and I will speak! According to Psalm 84:11, You are my sun and shield. You give me grace and glory. Thank You for Your willingness and Your power to help. There is no good thing that You would withhold from me. Because I trust in You, I have the power to prosper in this battle for *(insert your loved one's name)*'s life. I have the victory that overcomes the world.

Father, let Isaiah 61:1 prevail in *(insert your loved one's name)*'s life. The Spirit of the Lord has anointed Jesus to proclaim liberty to the captives and the opening of the prison to them that are bound. Second Corinthians 3:17 (AMPC) declares, *"Now the Lord is the Spirit, and where the Spirit of the Lord is, there is liberty (emancipation from bondage, freedom)."* I pray that *(insert your loved one's name)* would walk in liberty and seek Your precepts. As Your truth is revealed to *(insert your loved one's name)*, John 8:32 operates. They will know the truth, and the truth will make them free.

In Jesus' name, I focus on Your faithfulness. Sarah received strength to conceive Isaac because she counted You faithful (Heb. 11:11). I choose to do the same and develop my trust in You. I consider You to be more trustworthy than what the evidence says about this situation.

Father, Your truth is more powerful than any lie the enemy could implant into *(insert your loved one's name)*'s thinking. I pray that Your truth be exalted in his/her understanding.

I ask You, according to Isaiah 44:3-4, to pour Your water, Spirit, and blessing on *(insert your loved one's name)*. They shall spring up as among the grass, as willows by the water courses.

You made known Your ways to Moses and Your acts to the children of Israel (Ps. 103:7). I ask You, in Jesus' name, to make Your ways and acts known to *(insert your loved one's name)*.

# BUILD YOUR FAITH

### MATTHEW 17:20

*So Jesus said to them, "Because of your unbelief; for assuredly, I say to you, if you have faith as a mustard seed, you will say to this mountain, 'Move from here to there,' and it will move; and nothing will be impossible for you."*

### MATTHEW 21:21-22

*So Jesus answered and said to them, "Assuredly, I say to you, if you have faith and do not doubt, you will not only do what was done to the fig tree, but also if you say to this mountain, 'Be removed and be cast into the sea,' it will be done. And whatever things you ask in prayer, believing, you will receive."*

## PSALM 37:40

*And the Lord shall help them and deliver them; He shall deliver them from the wicked, and save them, because they trust in Him.*

## PSALM 84:11-12

*For the Lord God is a sun and shield; the Lord will give grace and glory; no good thing will He withhold from those who walk uprightly. O Lord of hosts, blessed is the man who trusts in You!*

# GOD, WILL YOU HELP ME?

### 2 PETER 3:9 (AMP)

*The Lord does not delay [as though He were unable to act] and is not slow about His promise, as some count slowness, but is [extraordinarily] patient toward you, **not wishing for any to perish but for all to come to repentance.***

Rosa kneeled at the altar, choking back her emotion. Her lips tried to form the words of a prayer, but the despair of her situation flooded her heart. Her mind raced as she replayed the words that had brought such a whirlwind of turmoil. "Mom. I'm at the airport in Columbia. I've been arrested for drug trafficking. Help me!"

The fear twisted her stomach into knots as she thought of her daughter in a Columbian prison. Rosa barely had the funds to pay for her own utilities this month and put groceries on the table for the five-year-old grandson she was raising. She didn't have money for a lawyer or any way to help her daughter.

The tumultuous fear was interrupted by surges of anger. One moment, Rosa was crying over her daughter's predicament. Then, the fear was replaced with fury! *How could she do this to us? I was trying to help her get on her feet. I am raising her son and giving her a place to live. When will she ever change?*

The turmoil was more than Rosa could handle. She was relieved when the pastor had opened the altar, but now, as she found herself trying to ask God for help, her mind slammed on the brakes. The same questions that infuriated her stood up against her prayer. *How can I ask God to help her? She did this to herself! She lied again! How many times did she say she was going to change but went right back to her lying, scheming ways? God is probably through with her.*

So, she began to beg God, but her feeble pleas sounded empty and hollow. With tears and despair, she agonized at the altar. When she finally wiped her tears, she was spent. Physically and emotionally exhausted, Rosa stood to her feet. Her head hung in shame as she walked down the church aisle. She felt like a failure as a mother. She couldn't even talk God into helping her daughter.

Sadly, many people who love God with all their hearts experience this same desperation. But it is because they lack the knowledge of God, who He is, and how He responds in times of need.

## HOSEA 4:6

*My people are destroyed for lack of knowledge.*

You must be certain of God's love and willingness to save so you can pray effectively. God wants your loved one to accept Jesus as Lord and walk free of Satan's power because as deeply as you love them, God loves them more. The Bible declares, *"For God so loved the world that He gave His only begotten Son, that whoever believes in Him should not perish but have everlasting life. For God did not send His Son into the world to condemn the world, but that the world through Him might be saved"* (John 3:16-17).

# SHE WORSHIPED HIM, SAYING, "LORD, HELP ME!"

The Canaanite woman didn't have a covenant right to approach Jesus, but she had confidence He would help her. She requested an intervention on behalf of her daughter.

## MATTHEW 15:22-28

*And behold, a woman of Canaan came from that region and cried out to Him, saying, "Have mercy on me, O Lord, Son of David! My daughter is severely demon-possessed." But He answered her not a word.*

*And His disciples came and urged Him, saying, "Send her away, for she cries out after us."*

*But He answered and said, "I was not sent except to the lost sheep of the house of Israel."*

*Then **she came and worshiped Him, saying, "Lord, help me!"***

*But He answered and said, "It is not good to take the children's bread and throw it to the little dogs."*

*And she said, "Yes, Lord, yet even the little dogs eat the crumbs which fall from their masters' table."*

*Then Jesus answered and said to her, "O woman, great is your faith! Let it be to you as you desire." And her daughter was healed from that very hour.*

She made a connection to the intervention available through Jesus Christ. The Canaanite woman went against the odds to fight in faith for her daughter's life. She stood against the circumstance and activated the power of God with her faith, bringing God's intervention on the scene. Your confidence in God's love will motivate you to stand like this!

## TO SEEK AND SAVE

Jesus came to save sinners! Jesus declared of Himself, *"for the Son of Man has come to seek and to save that which was lost"* (Luke 19:10 AMP). First Timothy 1:15 says, *"This is a faithful saying and worthy of all acceptance, that Christ Jesus came into the world to save sinners."*

Jesus has a history of saving people who were beyond help. When Jesus encountered the man possessed by a legion of demons, Jesus intervened.

### MARK 5:2-8

*And when He had come out of the boat, immediately there met Him out of the tombs a man with an unclean spirit, who had his dwelling among the tombs; and no one could bind him, not even with chains, because he had often been bound with shackles and chains. And the chains had been pulled apart by him, and the shackles broken in pieces; neither could anyone tame him. And always, night and day, he was in the mountains and in the tombs, crying out and cutting himself with stones.*

*When he saw Jesus from afar, he ran and worshiped Him. And he cried out with a loud voice and said, "What have I to do with You, Jesus, Son of the Most High God? I implore You by God that You do not torment me."*

*For He said to him, "Come out of the man, unclean spirit!"*

Even though the man's family and friends could not help him, Jesus went out of His way to set this man free. How much more will Jesus work on our behalf as we stand on His Word and worship Him for His faithfulness?

## A NOTORIOUS SINNER FORGIVEN

Another example is the woman who was a wicked sinner who was washing Jesus' feet with her tears and wiping His feet dry with the hair of her head.

### LUKE 7:37-39, 47-48 (AMPC)

*And behold, a woman of the town who was an especially wicked sinner, when she learned that He was reclining at table in the Pharisee's house, brought an alabaster flask of ointment (perfume).*

*And standing behind Him at His feet weeping, she began to wet His feet with [her] tears; and she wiped them with the hair of her head and kissed His feet [affectionately] and anointed them with the ointment (perfume).*

*Now when the Pharisee who had invited Him saw it, he said to himself, If this Man were a prophet, He would surely know who and what sort of woman this is who is touching Him—for she is a notorious sinner (a social outcast, devoted to sin).*

*…Therefore I tell you, her sins, many [as they are], are forgiven her—because she has loved much. But he who is forgiven little loves little. And He said to her, Your sins are forgiven!*

You can put your confidence in the willingness of our Heavenly Father and our Savior, Jesus Christ, to help. God is on the salvation side. Jesus came to find them and rescue the lost. Knowing God's position will keep us from begging or pleading with God to do something He already desires to do. Let's pray from that position.

## YOUR INTERVENTION PRAYER

Heavenly Father, I come to You in Jesus' name with confidence that You desire to save *(insert your loved one's name)* and set him/her free from all destruction. Your Word reveals You are patient, and I thank You for that patience with *(insert your loved one's name)*. God, thank You for loving *(insert your loved one's name)* so much You gave Your only begotten Son that whoever believes on Him shall not perish.

You sent Jesus to seek and save *(insert your loved one's name)*. According to Isaiah 55:7, You want *(insert your loved one's name)* to turn away from the things that are destroying his/her life and turn to You. I break the root of rebellion that the enemy has planted in his/her heart. According to Proverbs 21:1, the heart of the king is in Your hand, and You can turn it. I ask You to turn my loved one's heart toward You.

Hebrews 10 tells me that Jesus came to this earth to open the new and living way for *(insert your loved one's name)* to be saved from sin. Father, I rejoice that You love *(insert your loved one's name)* more than I do. I choose to pray with my focus on Your kindness and willingness to work in the life of *(insert your loved one's name)*.

I ask You to reveal to me how deeply You care for *(insert your loved one's name)*. You said that the plans You have for his/her future are good plans with an end and expectation. I want to pray from Your perspective. I want my prayers to agree with You so that You can work easily with the requests I make and petitions I submit.

I celebrate Your love for me. Thank You for allowing me to have *(insert your loved one's name)* in my life. I will not fear having him/her taken from me by any force of destruction. In line with 1 Corinthians 13, I believe that love never fails. Let Your love flow through me to strengthen me to stand in faith for *(insert your loved one's name)*.

## BUILD YOUR FAITH

### 2 PETER 3:9 (VOICE)

*Now the Lord is not slow about enacting His promise—slow is how some people want to characterize it—no, He is not slow but patient and merciful to you,* **not wanting anyone to be destroyed,** *but wanting everyone to turn away from following his own path and to turn toward God's.*

## ACTS 16:30-32

*And he brought them out and said, "Sirs, what must I do to be saved?" So they said, **"Believe on the Lord Jesus Christ, and you will be saved, you and your household."** Then they spoke the word of the Lord to him and to all who were in his house.*

## ACTS 13:38-39

*Therefore let it be known to you, brethren, that through this Man is preached to you the forgiveness of sins; and by Him everyone who believes is justified from all things from which you could not be justified by the law of Moses.*

## JEREMIAH 29:11

*For I know the thoughts that I think toward you, says the Lord, thoughts of peace and not of evil, **to give you a future and a hope**.*

# THE BASIS OF YOUR CLAIM

To avoid praying the problem, you need to lay the foundation of your approach to God. Your heart should be full of answers from the Word of God about the salvation of your loved ones instead of the problems you see in their lives.

If your heart is full of worry and desperation, you will bring forth that desperation in prayer. Praying the problem is not the way Jesus taught us to pray. In Mark 11:24 (KJV), He said, *"What things soever ye desire, when ye pray, believe that ye receive them, and ye shall have them."* The Lord already knows what you need before you ask Him. The way you approach God is to come to Him on the foundation of His Word.

If you have ever placed a claim with an insurance company, you know that any claim must have a foundation, an agreement that the insurance will cover any damage or replace the broken part. If anything happens to it, then you can report a claim to the insurance company.

If you try to place a claim for something that is not insured, it will not be covered. You may think you are covered for certain things only to find out you are not. The paperwork will show that there is no basis for that claim.

You must consult God's Word to locate what He has already said He would do about helping your family members. When you find out what He put in the covenant, you don't have to convince God to do something.

Instead, you find yourself working with His established will to intervene in your situation.

A *claim* is "a demand for something that is yours by right or promised to you by legal contract." The basis of your claim is the will of God. You are asking in line with His will.

## 2 PETER 3:9 (KJV)

*The Lord is not slack concerning his promise, as some men count slackness; but is longsuffering to us-ward, not willing that any should perish, but that all should come to repentance.*

The word *promise* in the Bible refers to "a covenant provision, a term of the contract." It is something already available. When you find the promises of God, you discover what He has already made yours in the covenant. Then, you have the legal right to use your faith and receive it.

The will of God is that all people should come to repentance! God wants every person to be saved. So, praying, "Lord, please save them," puts God at a disadvantage. He has already stated His will. He wants them to receive salvation more than we want it. You don't need to twist His arm or talk Him into the idea.

God already provided all that they need to be saved. The blood of Jesus is available to cleanse them from sin, and the price has been paid to free them from the penalty of sin. The Lord is waiting on your loved one to turn to Him and access what He has made available in salvation.

So, how can you set up an intervention like the Shunammite woman? You come to God based on His covenant with you. You use covenant language and deal with the situation based on what is legally yours in the spiritual realm by saying, "Lord, I thank You that You provided all that is needed for my loved one to be saved. Jesus died on the cross for them and poured out His blood to set them free. I pray for that salvation to become clear to them. Let them see the price Jesus paid and accept Jesus as their Lord."

There is a legal way for you to approach God. You can petition God on the terms of the salvation that He has provided.

# FIND THE PROMISE

I was saved at age 23 after eight years of drug addiction, prostitution, and crime. I entered my walk with God not knowing anything about the Bible, church, or God. Prayer was something new to me. When I first learned to pray, I was praying for my needs. I needed everything! Little by little, I began to gain confidence as I talked to God, asking Him to help me with the various situations in my life. But after my petitions were made, I fell silent. What now?

The breakthrough in prayer and my relationship with God came from taking the Bible into my prayer time. Amazing! The Holy Spirit took me to certain verses of the Bible that fueled my conversation with God. I learned to feed on those scriptures morning after morning. As I did, my prayers shifted. There was a release of power in my prayers.

As I grew in the Lord, I realized my responsibility to pray for the other people in my life. I learned to pray for the leaders in my nation as the Bible instructs in 1 Timothy 2:1-2. People in my church and immediate family also appeared on my radar, and I searched the Scriptures for verses to fuel my supplications.

Prayer is not like gambling or a game of chance. Prayer is a vital part of our relationship with our Heavenly Father. When we pray for other people, we are partnering with God and believing for His will to be done. Our confidence in prayer originates from the promise we find in His Word.

## 1 JOHN 5:14-15 (AMPC)

*And this is the confidence (the assurance, the privilege of boldness) which we have in Him: [we are sure] that if we ask anything (make any request) according to His will (in agreement with His own plan), He listens to and hears us.*

*And if (since) we [positively] know that He listens to us in whatever we ask, we also know [with settled and absolute knowledge] that we have [granted us as our present possessions] the requests made of Him.*

Whether you are praying for your child, spouse, mother, or sibling, God will lead you to a specific promise. Then, you must meditate on the promise. The confidence grows because you know you are asking in line with God's desire for their lives.

## JOSHUA 1:8

*This Book of the Law shall not depart from your mouth, but you shall meditate in it day and night, that you may observe to do according to all that is written in it. For then you will make your way prosperous, and then you will have good success.*

The word *meditate* means "to imagine, ponder, or mutter." We meditate on God's Word by speaking it to ourselves. This keeps our mind occupied with the Word. Then, we begin to see the image of the promise etched into our innermost being.

Can you see your loved ones with their hands lifted to the Lord, calling on the name of Jesus? Can you imagine their faces shining with the glory of God as they sing praises to God? Can you picture them preaching, serving as a greeter or usher in the church, or singing in the choir? If not, don't despair. Just turn back to the Word and feed on it some more. Put the Word in front of your eyes!

### PSALM 1:2-3 (AMPC)

*But his delight and desire are in the law of the Lord, and on His law (the precepts, the instructions, the teachings of God) he habitually meditates (ponders and studies) by day and by night. And he shall be like a tree firmly planted [and tended] by the streams of water, ready to bring forth its fruit in its season; its leaf also shall not fade or wither; and everything he does shall prosper [and come to maturity].*

God's Word is His will. So, we can be confident when we have His Word on the subject. We have confidence that He hears us as we call for the salvation of our loved ones, and He responds with His help. God wants us to approach Him with this kind of confidence!

# YOUR INTERVENTION PRAYER

Father, in Jesus' name, I thank You that You hear me. As I pray for *(insert your loved one's name),* You are listening to my prayer and moving to answer those prayers. Lord, Your Word says Your ear is open to my cry. When I seek Your face, You will hear from Heaven and answer my prayer. I have confidence in You.

Father, it is Your will for *(insert your loved one's name)* to walk in the light of Your Word. I pray for them to see Your light. I ask You to shine the truth brighter than any darkness surrounding him/her. I break the authority of Satan and pray against any lies of witchcraft, the occult, astrology, and dark arts. Let those lies be exposed and satanic curses be broken. I pray for the blood of Jesus to set *(insert your loved one's name)* free from bondages that came through the door of satanic movies, games, or books.

In Matthew 13:15, You said if *(insert your loved one's name)* could see and hear, then he/she could understand and be converted. I pray for *(insert your loved one's name)* to see Your love, Your truth, and the perfect plan for his/her life. I release the power of Psalm 91:15 to be available to *(insert your loved one's name)*—as they call on You, Lord, You will answer them and be with them. You will deliver and honor *(insert your loved one's name).* Compel *(insert your loved one's name)* by Your Spirit to hope in You and call on Your name.

Father, I will not fear losing *(insert your loved one's name).* I will not fear that *(insert your loved one's name)* will die in his/her sin. I will not fear because I have confidence in You. I have confidence in Your Word.

I rejoice because I know *(insert your loved one's name)* is being saved. I rejoice because *(insert your loved one's name)* is seeing the truth about why Jesus died on the cross. I praise You that *(insert your loved one's name)* is receiving the free gift of salvation!

## BUILD YOUR FAITH

### PSALM 91:15 (KJV)

*He shall call upon me, and I will answer him: I will be with him in trouble; I will deliver him, and honour him.*

### 2 CHRONICLES 7:14 (KJV)

*If my people, which are called by my name, shall humble them-selves, and pray, and seek my face, and turn from their wicked ways; then will I hear from heaven, and will forgive their sin, and will heal their land.*

### MATTHEW 13:15

*For the hearts of this people have grown dull. Their ears are hard of hearing, And their eyes they have closed, Lest they should see with their eyes and hear with their ears, Lest they should understand with their hearts and turn, So that I should heal them.*

## 1 JOHN 5:14 (AMPC)

*And this is the confidence (the assurance, the privilege of boldness) which we have in Him: [we are sure] that if we ask anything (make any request) according to His will (in agreement with His own plan), He listens to and hears us.*

# HOW TO WORK *WITH* GOD'S WILL

M any pray as if they are trying to talk God into saving their loved ones, and they feel frustrated about it. They are trying to convince God, but the Lord is already convinced! If I beg my husband to marry me, he is at a disadvantage. As much as he loves me and would do anything for me, he can do nothing to be *more* married to me than he already is. Even if we stood before a preacher and spoke our wedding vows again, it wouldn't make us any more married than we already are. This kind of prayer lacks the faith to open the situation for God's intervention.

## LUKE 19:10 (GW)

*Indeed, the Son of Man has come to seek and to save people who are lost.*

God is already 100 percent willing to save our loved ones. When we pray with faith in God's will to save, we pray with courage and expectation. Before we pray, let's settle the will of God firmly in our hearts.

## ACTS 10:38

*How God anointed Jesus of Nazareth with the Holy Spirit and with power, who went about doing good and healing all who were oppressed by the devil, for God was with Him.*

It is God's will, and He has already made salvation available in Jesus Christ. God is looking for a covenant partner in your family who will stand in the gap to defend against the enemy's attack. He is looking for someone to say, "Lord, I will be the one whom You can call on. I am Yours to command. Do you need me to pray for Aunt Nancy? I will focus on Aunt Nancy in prayer."

Then, God can come to you and say, "Why don't you ask Me to do more for Aunt Nancy? Why don't you ask Me to open the eyes of her understanding?"

So, you begin to ask, "Lord, I pray that You can open the eyes of her understanding." You may think, *Well, God can do anything He wants. So, why do I need to pray for that?* But that is not how God has chosen to operate on the earth. God is sovereign in that He is all-powerful, but God delegated the authority on the earth to mankind. The Lord gave us the right to choose, and He won't violate our will. God is just.

## JAMES 5:16-18

*The effective, fervent prayer of a righteous man avails much. Elijah was a man with a nature like ours, and he prayed earnestly that it would not rain; and it did not rain on the land for three years and six months. And he prayed again, and the heaven gave rain, and the earth produced its fruit.*

Elijah prayed that it would rain because God told him that it would rain (1 Kings 18:1). God's covenant representative on earth got into an agreement with the will of God and prayed in line with it. Elijah gave God legal access into the earth to do that thing.

If God could have orchestrated His will in the situation without the prayers of Elijah, why did the Holy Spirit use this example to illustrate the effect of our prayers?

Our prayers avail much. The Amplified Bible, Classic Edition says, "*The earnest (heartfelt, continued) prayer of a righteous man makes tremendous power available [dynamic in its working].*"

Young's Literal Translation says: "*Very strong is a working supplication of a righteous man.*"

The Moffatt New Translation says: "*The prayer of the righteous has a powerful effect.*"

God's power is available, and we activate it as His representatives. We voice the effectual, fervent prayer. We are instruments that God can use. He can move through the situation and cause His power to be made available.

## PARTNERS IN PRAYER

The role you take in intervention prayer is one of partnership. As you pray in agreement with what God wants for your loved ones, you join forces with God to see His perfect plan unfold. If you get your prayer cues from the One who knows exactly what will solve the problem, it is just a matter of time until you see results.

## ZECHARIAH 10:1 (KJV)

*Ask ye of the Lord rain in the time of the latter rain; so the Lord shall make bright clouds, and give them showers of rain, to every one grass in the field.*

In prayer, you activate God's will in the lives of your loved ones by using your authority and faith to give God legal access to intervene. We see this portrayed when God spoke to Elijah to tell Ahab that it would not rain. He had the knowledge of what God wanted in the situation. Yet, Elijah prayed earnestly that it would not rain.

## JAMES 5:17-18 (NLT)

*Elijah was as human as we are, and yet when he prayed earnestly that no rain would fall, none fell for three and a half years! Then, when he prayed again, the sky sent down rain and the earth began to yield its crops.*

Elijah prayed in line with God's will, which authorized God to move in the situation. God worked *with* and *through* Elijah to bring His will to pass in that circumstance. Similarly, God clearly outlines His will for your family members in His Word. You participate with God through prayer to see His will brought to pass. You ask according to God's will, and He answers according to your faith-filled prayers.

We must remember this: God's hand is not moved just because of a need. He doesn't answer according to the abundance of our tears or the severity of the situation. God's grace is accessed by our faith. Romans 4:16 says, "*Therefore it is of faith that it might be according to grace, so that the promise might be sure to all the seed.*" Faith is our part!

The Lord works in harmony with His Word that is working in us. God *"is able to do exceedingly abundantly above all that we ask or think, according to the power that works in us"* (Eph. 3:20).

You must stand in faith with your prayer petitions established on the Word of God. If you are praying in faith, you are not desperate, afraid, worried, or grieving. You refuse to allow the circumstances to govern how you think, feel, or talk. You pray with joy, peace, and thankfulness and go through your day saying, "Thank You, Jesus, for the salvation of *(insert your loved one's name)*." Let's pray!

## YOUR INTERVENTION PRAYER

Father, You are good! In Jesus' name, I praise You for Your mercy and loving-kindness. It is Your will to save *(insert your loved one's name)*. I pray in line with Your will and declare the light of the gospel is brightly shining to *(insert your loved one's name)*.

I enforce Christ's victory over every plan of the enemy and declare no weapon formed against them shall be able to prosper. I pray for the path my loved one is walking to be filled with the light of God. Send laborers across their path to speak words of truth that dispel the darkness and turn them toward the plan You have for them. Direct them away from wrong influences and deliver them from evil.

I break the stronghold of shame from *(insert your loved one's name)*'s life. Unravel the web of deceit that shame has used to bind them. Lord, may they know how faithful You are to forgive us. If we confess our sins,

You are faithful and just to forgive our sins and to cleanse us from all unrighteousness (1 John 1:9). You will have compassion on *(insert your loved one's name)*; You will subdue their iniquities and cast all their sins into the depth of the sea (Micah 7:19).

I refrain my voice from weeping and my eyes from tears because I believe *(insert your loved one's name)* shall come again from the land of the enemy. Thank You that there is hope in the future of *(insert your loved one's name)* and *(insert your loved one's name)* shall return (Jer. 31:16-17). I believe they will be like the prodigal son who came to himself and returned to his father's house.

Father, I ask You to draw *(insert your loved one's name)* to repent. Manifest Your mercy and love to them in supernatural ways. According to Joel 2:11-13, let him/her turn to You with all their heart and return to Your ways because You are slow to anger and of great kindness. Thank You for Your mercy!

## BUILD YOUR FAITH

### HEBREWS 4:16

*Let us therefore come boldly to the throne of grace, that we may obtain mercy and find grace to help in time of need.*

## JAMES 5:15-16 (AMPC)

*And the prayer [that is] of faith will save him who is sick, and the Lord will restore him; and if he has committed sins, he will be forgiven. Confess to one another therefore your faults (your slips, your false steps, your offenses, your sins) and pray [also] for one another, that you may be healed and restored [to a spiritual tone of mind and heart]. The earnest (heartfelt, continued) prayer of a righteous man makes tremendous power available [dynamic in its working].*

## EPHESIANS 1:17-20 (WET)

*That the God of our Lord Jesus Christ, the Father of the glory, might give to you a spirit of wisdom and revelation in the sphere of a full knowledge of Him, the eyes of your heart being in an enlightened state with a view to your knowing what is the hope of His calling, what is the wealth of the glory of His inheritance in the saints, and what is the superabounding greatness of His inherent power to us who are believing ones as measured by the operative energy of the manifested strength of His might, which might was operative in the Christ when He raised Him from among the dead and seated Him at His right hand in the heavenly places.*

# WEEK TWO

## INTERVENTION STORY:
# HE'S STILL LISTENING

Juanita saw the Lord work a supernatural intervention in her son's life. It was a stand of faith in which she found God faithful to work with her in prayer. Many times, the Lord directed her how to pray, specifically in situations where she was clueless about the details of what was going on in his life.

Juanita says, "I did my best to raise my children in the truth, trusting God that all my children would walk with Him. I had no idea that one would go down a path that was so daunting. My son chose to live a life of drugs, alcohol, and homosexuality."

Although her son had been brought up in church and was involved in the youth group and music ministry, his life took a different direction after high school. He moved to another state, and Juanita was unaware of the dangerous decisions her son was making until she received a desperate phone call.

Juanita explains, "I received a phone call late in the night. My son opened up, telling me how he was living. As his mom, my heart was aching as I rehearsed the things he told me, but as a believer, I wanted to help him find God's help and freedom. I wanted to give him scripture that would help him and say, 'Let's repent and get right with God.' Instead, I asked him, 'Do you want to live this way?'"

He answered, "No."

Juanita says, "I took that word 'no' and kept it in my heart. My son was in bondage, and as his mom, I wanted to fix him. This was new to me. When my son called, I wanted to minister to him, but the Lord told me to love him. I said, 'Lord, I do love him!'"

God explained, saying, "Love him *through* it."

Juanita says, "I thought I knew what to do until I realized I didn't know what to do! I was trying to pray for him while not really knowing *how* to pray about his situation. My heart as a 'mom' was getting in the way."

## PROVERBS 3:5-6 (AMPC)

*Lean on, trust in, and be confident in the Lord with all your heart and mind and do not rely on your own insight or understanding. In all your ways know, recognize, and acknowledge Him, and He will direct and make straight and plain your paths.*

Juanita realized that she didn't have a natural understanding of how to pray for her son, but she knew the Lord did! The Lord knew what was in his heart, the influences that were motivating him, and the key that would unlock her son's heart.

She said, "I was trying to rely on my own understanding, but I had no idea how to pray for what my son was facing. I had to learn to love my son *through* everything he was doing. He knew right from wrong, but he didn't need me to point that out to him. He needed to be loved with God's love. I finally surrendered and let God show me how to love him. Every time my son called, I listened with God's love—not as a mom and without using scriptures. We just had a conversation. After we hung up from the phone call, I would pray for him."

Then, the Lord directed Juanita to do something specific. She said, "An idea rose up in my spirit. *Hang a picture of him on the wall.* So, I did. Next, an instruction came to me. 'Point your finger at his picture and call him what he is and not what he is doing.' It was like a light shining in my heart. I knew what to do!"

## ROMANS 4:17

*Calls those things which do not exist as though they did.*

Juanita said, "I pointed my finger at the picture on the wall and declared, 'Son, you are saved and filled with the Holy Spirit. You are in church, fulfilling God's plan for your life!' The stand of faith continued, but the Lord was faithful to encourage me along the way. One night, during a prayer meeting in my church, my pastor wrote something on a piece of paper and handed it to me. On the paper was written, *He's still listening.* My heart was strengthened! On another occasion, as he was ministering during an evening service, my pastor told me there was a ministering angel there with my son. Again, the Lord provided fuel for my stand of faith."

The Lord continued to work with Juanita in prayer, providing encouragement as she needed it. She explains, "A year went by, and one day when I opened up my Bible, that piece of paper with the words *He's still listening* fell onto my lap. I looked at it and heard in my spirit, 'Tape it to the back of his picture on the wall.' So, I did, and I added to my list of what I was calling him. The turnaround didn't happen overnight. I would walk by his picture, stop and point my finger, and call him what he is and not what he was doing."

There were days when it didn't seem like her prayers were getting answered, and it was becoming disheartening at times. Then, she would stand up and say, "My son is worth it! His freedom is worth the effort it takes to stand in faith!" Juanita declared God's promises over her son again and again. She refused to give up on him. She learned to love her son *through it* for the next few years as she continued intervening for his life.

Juanita says, "I will never forget the day when I got a phone call, saying, 'Mom, I want to come home!' I shouted, '*Yes!* Come home, son. Our door is wide open for you!' He came home, and we wrapped our arms around him and loved him! During the time I stood in prayer for him, I kept imagining him standing with his hands up and surrendering to God. Let me tell you! *I got to see him standing with his hands up, surrendering to God!*

"Since that time, the Lord has restored my son's life. He is working in ministry, married to a beautiful young lady, and has two children. Today, my son is fulfilling the plan of God for his life! I am thankful for all the teachings from God's Word that have helped me to learn how to stand in faith and pray accurately. I am so grateful to the Holy Spirit for helping me pray specifically. When it seems like you are not seeing the changes you're praying for, don't give up! Keep standing with God in prayer for your loved ones. Trust God and call them what God says they are. It shall come to pass!"

## DAY 8

# YOUR RIGHT TO RESIST

What gives you the authority to influence this situation in prayer? What legal stand do you have in the spiritual battle that is taking place in your loved ones' lives? To answer those questions, you must understand God's delegated authority system.

In the beginning, God delegated dominion to mankind. When Adam sinned, he delivered his God-given dominion to the control of Satan. But Jesus came as a Man, born into the earth legally, to regain the dominion Adam had lost. The Lord spoke of His legal entry through birth, comparing it to the illegal entrance made by Satan.

### JOHN 10:1-2

*Most assuredly, I say to you, he who does not enter the sheepfold by the door, but climbs up some other way, the same is a thief and a robber. But he who enters by the door is the shepherd of the sheep.*

Jesus, the Second Person of the Godhead, came in the form and fashion of a man. That doesn't mean that He pretended to be a man. Jesus *legally* became a human being so that He could *legally* regain the dominion delegated to men.

## PHILIPPIANS 2:7 (AMPC)

*But stripped Himself [of all privileges and rightful dignity], so as to assume the guise of a servant (slave), in that He became like men and was born a human being.*

Another reason that Jesus took on flesh and blood was so He could taste death for every man. Legally, His blood—sinless, innocent, and holy—would qualify to set us free from the legal demand that death (even spiritual death) had on us. Because the wages of sin is death, Jesus died in our place.

## HEBREWS 2:9 (KJV)

*But we see Jesus, who was made a little lower than the angels for the suffering of death, crowned with glory and honour; that he by the grace of God should taste death for every man.*

Jesus' death as a willing sacrifice displayed the love God has for us. Jesus understood that God wanted the relationship with mankind completely restored. We see these words Jesus spoke to the Heavenly Father:

## HEBREWS 10:5-7

*Therefore, when He came into the world, He said: "Sacrifice and offering You did not desire, but a body You have prepared for Me. In burnt offerings and sacrifices for sin You had no pleasure. Then I said, 'Behold, I have come—in the volume of the book it is written of Me—to do Your will, O God.'"*

Jesus came, knowing that the sacrifice He would make would include His death and separation from God. He was willing to endure the punishment we deserved so that we could return to our intended relationship with God, including the restoration of our authority to rule and reign with God.

## ROMANS 5:17 (KJV)

*For if by one man's offence death reigned by one; much more they which receive abundance of grace and of the gift of righteousness shall reign in life by one, Jesus Christ.*

# OUR RIGHT TO GOVERN IN JESUS' NAME

So, when Jesus died on the cross, He regained the authority Adam had lost. Because of Jesus' obedience to the cross, God highly exalted Him and delegated a name of honor and authority to Jesus. The name refers to the title and position God has given Jesus above every governing force on earth.

## PHILIPPIANS 2:9-11

*Therefore God also has highly exalted Him and given Him the name which is above every name, that at the name of Jesus every knee should bow, of those in heaven, and of those on earth, and of those under the earth, and that every tongue should confess that Jesus Christ is Lord, to the glory of God the Father.*

Today, Jesus holds the highest position of authority in the universe. He exercises this dominion as a glorified man—all God and all man!

## 1 TIMOTHY 2:5

*For there is one God and one Mediator between God and men,*
*the Man Christ Jesus.*

Jesus referred to Himself as "the Son of Man" because He wanted to emphasize His legal position as a human being. Jesus was completely the Son of God. Yet, because He came in the form of a human being, Jesus was legally the Son of Man, also.

In the same manner, we are human beings, but through our faith in Jesus Christ, we are legally children of God. Our restored relationship with God includes the authority in Jesus' name. In John 14, 15, and 16, Jesus instructed His disciples (including you and me) to ask in His name, promising that the Father will respond as if Jesus Himself is making the request.

So, let's answer the questions: "What gives you authority?" and "What legal stand do you have?" Your faith in Christ provides you with His authority, and your legal stand is that of one sent by Jesus to represent His will. You can use this authority to represent the will of God in the lives of your loved ones!

## YOUR INTERVENTION PRAYER

I take the weapons of my warfare (2 Cor. 10:4-5), which are mighty through God. I pull down the strongholds of addiction, fear, and shame.

Lord, whatever thought process is holding *(insert your loved one's name)*'s mind in this lifestyle, I pull it down. That stronghold will no longer prevail against God's truth. I cast down every imagination that works in *(insert your loved one's name)*'s mind. Every lie of the enemy that has exalted itself against the knowledge of God, I cast down.

I stand on Jeremiah 24:7 (NIV), which says, *"I will give them a heart to know me, that I am the Lord. They will be my people, and I will be their God, for they will return to me with all their heart."* I pray for a softening of *(insert your loved one's name)*'s heart. I ask that You remove the hardness in their heart and, according to Psalm 51:10 (NIV), that You create in *(insert your loved one's name)* a clean heart and renew a steadfast spirit in them.

I am thankful that *(insert your loved one's name)* will not be prey or victim to the heathen (Ezek. 34:28), neither shall the beast of the land devour him/her. *(Insert your loved one's name)* will live in safety.

I thank You for Your Word. Let Your Word be a lamp to *(insert your loved one's name)*'s feet and light to his/her path. Father, I thank You that Your Word will not return void (Isa. 55: 11). Your Word will accomplish what it is sent to do. I send Your Word to *(insert your loved one's name)* and thank You for his/her salvation.

I praise You, Lord! I praise You for the light of Your Word that is leading *(insert your loved one's name)* into all truth. I thank You for the angels who are encamped around *(insert your loved one's name)* to protect him/her. I rejoice and am glad because Your Holy Spirit is speaking to (insert your loved one's name), and he/she is listening!

# BUILD YOUR FAITH

## MARK 16:15-18

*And He said to them, "Go into all the world and preach the gospel to every creature. He who believes and is baptized will be saved; but he who does not believe will be condemned. And these signs will follow those who believe: In My name they will cast out demons; they will speak with new tongues; they will take up serpents; and if they drink anything deadly, it will by no means hurt them; they will lay hands on the sick, and they will recover."*

## EZEKIEL 34:28

*And they shall no longer be a prey for the nations, nor shall beasts of the land devour them; but they shall dwell safely, and no one shall make them afraid.*

## ISAIAH 21:6

*For thus has the Lord said to me: "Go, set a watchman, Let him declare what he sees."*

## PSALM 147:11 (AMPC)

*The Lord takes pleasure in those who reverently and worshipfully fear Him, in those who hope in His mercy and loving-kindness.*

## DAY 9

# GOD'S LEGAL COVENANT

L egally, Jesus had authority over the wind and waves. He had the authority to operate on the earth in the dominion God originally intended mankind to operate. In Christ, we have legal authority too!

God won't do things illegally. Although Satan entered the Garden of Eden illegally and deceived Eve, that is not how God operates. God looked for a man with whom He could establish His legal covenant. Abraham was willing to be obedient and follow the instructions God gave him. Abraham's obedience was orchestrated through faith. Faith is taking God at His Word and acting on it. Abraham obeyed when God said to leave his country and family. Abraham obeyed when the Lord instructed him to offer his son, Isaac. God said, "Now, I see you will obey Me." Obedience was Abraham's part of the covenant.

Through the legal covenant, because Abraham had offered his son to God, the Lord now had legal access to give His Son, Jesus Christ. Redemption was legally established. Jesus fulfilled all legal requirements to redeem us. After His death, burial, and resurrection, Jesus said, *"All authority has been given to Me in heaven and on earth. Go therefore"* (Matt. 28:18-19). We legally represent Jesus with authorization to enforce His will, God's will, on the earth.

Jesus prepared His disciples for a fundamental change when He went to the cross. Jesus said, *"And whatever you ask in My name, that I will do, that the Father may be glorified in the Son"* (John 14:13). He continued in John 15:16, *"I chose you and appointed you that you should go and bear fruit, and that your fruit should remain, that whatever you ask the Father in My name He may give you."* Wow! Jesus delegated His name to represent Him. Jesus will back up what we ask in His name!

Wait! There is more!

## JOHN 16:23-24

*And in that day you will ask Me nothing. Most assuredly, I say to you, whatever you ask the Father in My name He will give you. Until now you have asked nothing in My name. Ask, and you will receive, that your joy may be full.*

The fullness of our joy is connected to asking in Jesus' name. We are authorized and instructed to *ask in Jesus' name!* The Wuest Expanded Translation says, *"Be constantly making request, and you shall receive, in order that your joy, having been filled completely full, might persist in that state of fullness in present time."*

God is a covenant-keeping God. We approach Him based on our covenant, using the name of Jesus to pray for God's will concerning the salvation of our family members. As we do, we operate in a legal authority that Satan can't resist! The devil won't understand our declarations of faith and can't comprehend what God is doing through our prayers because we are operating on a higher level.

So, we will not be moved into the emotional or mental arena. We are going to represent Jesus, declare the Word of God, and interact with God's legal standing of our covenant. With an understanding of God's delegated authority, let's see how to apply it in our intervention prayer.

# RESISTANCE IS NECESSARY

Do you remember the phrase from *Star Trek* that said, "Resistance is futile"? Today, many believers believe that "resistance is futile" where praying for their loved ones is concerned. They don't resist the enemy because they think it won't do any good. They give up hope and entertain thoughts of their loved one's arrest, overdose, or funeral. Without any resistance, the enemy runs full speed ahead into their loved one's life and wreaks havoc.

Police officers have delegated authority. They train to know how to respond when confronting a criminal. They practice resistance and learn specific strategies to use in each situation. When they respond to a call, the training takes over, redirecting their emotions and thoughts toward the strategy they practiced.

If Jesus is your Lord, you have delegated authority too. You must train to operate God's dominion against the criminal trying to take the life of your loved one. Even though your resistance is spiritual, you can practice strategies and know your response to every enemy attack. You must resist the devil, or he won't leave. You can exercise authority and work *with* God to pray for the things that grant Him access to your loved one's life.

Let's consider the story of a father who brought his son to Jesus.

### MARK 9:17-22

*Then one of the crowd answered and said, "Teacher, I brought You my son, who has a mute spirit. And wherever it seizes him, it throws him down; he foams at the mouth, gnashes his teeth, and becomes rigid. So I spoke to Your disciples, that they should cast it out, but they could not."*

*He answered him and said, "O faithless generation, how long shall I be with you? How long shall I bear with you? Bring him to Me." Then they brought him to Him. And when he saw Him, immediately the spirit convulsed him, and he fell on the ground and wallowed, foaming at the mouth.*

*So He asked his father, "How long has this been happening to him?"*

*And he said, "From childhood. And often he has thrown him both into the fire and into the water to destroy him. But if You can do anything, have compassion on us and help us."*

The boy was under the control of a strong, destructive force that tried to kill him by throwing him into the water or a raging fire. Without the intervention prayer of his father, the boy would have been helpless.

Keep this in mind when you grow weary of taking your place in prayer. You are providing a lifeline when you pray for them. You are resisting the plan of the devil to kill them, to destroy their futures. Your resistance is *working!*

We must confront the enemy in Jesus' name. The devil's stronghold cannot withstand God's power released through our faith. No meth, oxycontin, alcohol, porn, or lust can stand against the power of God's promise to save our loved ones! So, let's dig in our spiritual heels and resist!

# YOUR INTERVENTION PRAYER

In the name of Jesus, I take my place against the adversary. I stand against the plans of the devil to destroy *(insert your loved one's name)* and plead the blood of Jesus Christ over him/her. I call for the peace of God to calm every raging situation in their life and declare God's blessing over *(insert your loved one's name)*. Lord, bless their mind with clarity and their heart with hope.

I deal with the pain of past rejections and the fear of rejection. In the name of Jesus, I break the root of rejection and condemnation and declare freedom for *(insert your loved one's name)*. Jesus was despised and rejected by men so that *(insert your loved one's name)* would be redeemed.

I command Satan to release his hold on *(insert your loved one's name)*. I pray against every relationship that Satan is using to influence my loved one. Let wrong motives be revealed. Expose those who are lying to and manipulating *(insert your loved one's name)*.

I speak to the enemy's plans against *(insert your loved one's name)* to fail. Satan, get your hands off *(insert your loved one's name)* in the name of Jesus. I draw the bloodline around my loved one's life. Their life is God's territory because God promised to save my family. I raise the banner of God's love over him/her.

I break the lies and deception that have been used to blind *(insert your loved one's name)* to the truth of God's Word. The light of God's Word will prevail over the darkness. I surround *(insert your loved one's name)* with faith and love, calling for the light of God's Word to shine brightly in *(insert your loved one's name)*'s understanding.

Father, I ask You to prompt me to pray against any new devices the adversary may use against *(insert your loved one's name)*. Reveal the enemy's strategies and show me how to pray specifically against the weapons the devil uses on *(insert your loved one's name)*.

# BUILD YOUR FAITH

### LUKE 10:19

*Behold, I give you the authority to trample on serpents and scorpions, and over all the power of the enemy, and nothing shall by any means hurt you.*

### EPHESIANS 6:10-16

*Finally, my brethren, be strong in the Lord and in the power of His might. Put on the whole armor of God, that you may be able to stand against the wiles of the devil. For we do not wrestle against flesh and blood, but against principalities, against powers, against the rulers of the darkness of this age, against spiritual hosts of wickedness in the heavenly places. Therefore take up the whole armor of God, that you may be able to withstand in the evil day, and having done all, to stand.*

*Stand therefore, having girded your waist with truth, having put on the breastplate of righteousness, and having shod your feet with the preparation of the gospel of peace; above all, taking*

*the shield of faith with which you will be able to quench all the fiery darts of the wicked one.*

## ACTS 16:31 (AMPC)

*And they answered, Believe in the Lord Jesus Christ [give yourself up to Him, take yourself out of your own keeping and entrust yourself into His keeping] and you will be saved, [and this applies both to] you and your household as well.*

# YOU CAN STAND AGAINST

We act on God's will *and* on God's behalf when we resist the devil and his destruction in the lives of our loved ones. Second Corinthians 5:20 (AMPC) says, *"So we are Christ's ambassadors, God making His appeal as it were through us."* God is using the power of our faith and the authority of our voices to pray for His will. We are God's "go-between" to stand against the destruction of the enemy.

## NUMBERS 16:47-48

*Then Aaron took it as Moses commanded, and ran into the midst of the assembly; and already the plague had begun among the people. So he put in the incense and made atonement for the people. And he stood between the dead and the living; so the plague was stopped.*

Aaron stood with God's fire and stopped the plague's advancement. What a picture this provides for us! When we take our place in prayer, we stand against the forces of destruction with God's glory to drive the enemy back.

## EPHESIANS 6:11

*Put on the whole armor of God, that you may be able to stand against the wiles of the devil.*

What does it mean to stand against the "wiles" of the devil? The word *wiles* indicates "a plan or scheme, especially one used to outwit an opponent or achieve a specific end." You can put on the armor of God and stand against the plan the devil has launched in your loved one's life. For example, 2 Corinthians 4:3-4 reveals that the enemy is trying to *"blind the mind"* of your loved one from seeing the light of the gospel. You can stand against that plan.

## EPHESIANS 6:12-13

*For we do not wrestle **against** flesh and blood, but **against** principalities, **against** powers, **against** the rulers of the darkness of this age, **against** spiritual hosts of wickedness in the heavenly places. Therefore take up the whole armor of God, that you may be able to withstand in the evil day, and having done all, to stand.*

The word *against* is a word that describes "a face-to-face confrontation, a close-contact battle between two opponents." It is used repeatedly in this verse for emphasis. But don't be dismayed or intimidated! We stand! When we come against the adversary, we stand, and he falls.

The Bible assures us that when resistance is applied, the devil flees. First Peter 5:8-9 says, *"Be sober, be vigilant; because your adversary the devil walks about like a roaring lion, seeking whom he may devour. Resist him, steadfast in the faith."* James 4:7 instructs us, *"Therefore submit to God. Resist the devil and he will flee from you."* We are equipped to stand and resist the devil's plan to destroy our loved ones!

## EPHESIANS 6:14-16

*Stand therefore, having girded your waist with truth, having put on the breastplate of righteousness, and having shod your*

*feet with the preparation of the gospel of peace; above all, taking the shield of faith with which you will be able to quench all the fiery darts of the wicked one.*

The power of God in you is stronger than any addiction. The ability of God is more capable of delivering your loved one than the addiction is able to keep them bound.

But the power and ability of God must be applied by His representatives. You must stand and resist the devil for your loved ones because God wants them to turn to Him. God's will is that none should perish. It is always His will to save your loved ones, and His promise in 2 Peter 3:9 provides a firm foundation for your faith.

## 2 PETER 3:9 (AMPC)

*The Lord does not delay and is not tardy or slow about what He promises, according to some people's conception of slowness, but He is long-suffering (extraordinarily patient) toward you, not desiring that any should perish, but that all should turn to repentance.*

The Weymouth Translation says, "*His desire being that no one should perish, but that all should come to repentance.*"

The Bible in Basic English says, "*Not desiring the destruction of any, but that all may be turned from their evil ways.*"

God's Word Translation says, "*He doesn't want to destroy anyone, but He wants all people to have an opportunity to turn to Him and change the way they think and act.*"

# PROVIDING OPEN DOORS

God is willing to open the eyes of the understanding of your loved one. He will send forth laborers across their paths. With intervention prayers, you can cause their life to be so full of open doors that eventually, they will recognize they don't need to keep walking on the path of destruction. They will go through an open door, find God's answer, and turn to God.

When you pray for family members, God's covenant works like a tool or an instrument to guide your prayers.

## GENESIS 17:7 (KJV)

*And I will establish my covenant between me and thee and thy seed after thee in their generations for an everlasting covenant, to be a God unto thee, and to thy seed after thee.*

Isaac had not yet been born, but God talked to Abraham about the covenant He would establish with Abraham's children. So, to whom is the promise made? God promised Abraham that He would save his children, and God promised me He would establish His covenant with *my* children. The promise is made to me. It is not made to my kids; it is *about* my kids. But it is made *to* me! Since God promised me that He would save my kids, I have His Word on it.

I realize that every person must make a personal decision to accept Jesus Christ as their Lord, my family members included. But if my loved ones see God, His love for them, His salvation, they will want Him. It is the enemy who blinds the mind and deceives. Our intervention prayers are faith-filled tools that open their eyes and shine the light of the gospel of Jesus Christ into their hearts.

The promise of salvation of the children is made to the parents so that we can exert and release our faith regardless of how they may be acting. We can keep that faith connection even when they don't seem interested in going in God's direction. We continue coming to God based on what His Word says about that promise.

### ISAIAH 49:25

*But thus says the Lord: "Even the captives of the mighty shall be taken away, and the prey of the terrible be delivered; for I will contend with him who contends with you, and I will save your children."*

Believing God holds the door open, providing a definite connection for God to continue ministering to our loved ones. If the opportunity comes for you to worry, if you hear they are making bad decisions, release your faith, saying, "Father, I cast the care of that upon You. I take You at Your Word, Lord. You promised me that You would establish Your covenant with my children and with me. You would be a God to my children. I take You at Your Word."

### ISAIAH 54:13

*All your children shall be taught by the Lord, and great shall be the peace of your children.*

In this Old Testament declaration, God gives you a picture to hold in your heart. You can take this declaration and put it in your heart and mouth. The power that is within this promise will be released into your family. You apply the promise to your situation by speaking it. God's Word is voice-activated, so say, "I thank You, Father! Great shall be the peace of my children. My children shall be taught of the Lord."

## ISAIAH 54:13 (AMPC)

*And all your [spiritual] children shall be disciples [taught by the Lord and obedient to His will], and great shall be the peace and undisturbed composure of your children.*

You must use these verses to imprint an image on your heart. Maybe the situation has built an image of loss or fear in your heart. Perhaps the enemy plays mental videos of death and destruction in your mind. Maybe you have worried at night, imagining your child in handcuffs. Perhaps you have feared them dying of an overdose or being shot in a drug deal. If you look at the problems, you will see all the "what ifs" of the enemy.

You must let the Word of God be the video playing in your mind. See your children walking into church with their Bibles. See your children standing in church with the glory of God hovering over them. Imagine them leading the worship service, teaching in Sunday school, or laying hands on the sick! Whatever the plan of God for their life is, you must build an image that reflects it. See them living a good, solid life. Picture them in a solid marriage with a sound financial situation. Get that image so you don't let the enemy play his negative videos.

The Lord told Joshua, "*This Book of the Law shall not depart out of your mouth, but you shall meditate on it day and night, that you may observe and do according to all that is written in it. For then you shall make your way prosperous, and then you shall deal wisely and have good success*" (Joshua 1:8 AMPC).

Meditating on the Word builds the picture of what the Word declares. You need to meditate on the Word of God where the salvation of your loved ones is concerned. Meditate on God's promises until, in your perception, the promises become stronger than the problems.

Give voice to God's will and shine God's light into the darkness of addiction. Things will change because God's Word will not return empty. It will accomplish what it is sent to accomplish!

# YOUR INTERVENTION PRAYER

In the name of Jesus, I stand in faith for *(insert your loved one's name)* to walk in the light of God's Word. Father, I ask You to remove every barrier that would hinder them from hearing or receiving Your Word.

I break the stronghold of darkness that would try to blind *(insert your loved one's name)* from knowing the truth about Jesus Christ. I declare that the devil's plan is a weapon that will not prosper against *(insert your loved one's name)*. I rejoice in the plan of God for his/her life. I believe to see the goodness of God dominating their life. Father, sanctify them through Your truth!

I command that *(insert your loved one's name)* will not die but live and declare the works of the Lord (Ps. 118:17). Psalm 68:6 declares that God brings out those who are bound by chains. I thank You, Lord, that You are bringing *(insert your loved one's name)* out of the chains of addiction, destruction, and deception.

I thank You that, like a bird hovering, You will defend *(insert your loved one's name).* You will protect and deliver them. You will pass over and spare and preserve them (Isa. 31:5 AMPC).

Father, I ask You in Jesus' name to give *(insert your loved one's name)* the spirit of wisdom and revelation in the knowledge of Jesus Christ. I pray for the eyes of *(insert your loved one's name)*'s understanding to be fully flooded with light so that he/she will know the hope of Your calling and the riches of the glory of Your inheritance. Lord, I pray that *(insert your loved one's name)* will know the exceeding greatness of Your power toward us who believe according to the working of Your mighty power (Eph. 1:17-19).

## BUILD YOUR FAITH

### 1 JOHN 5:4 (AMP)

*For everyone born of God is victorious and overcomes the world; and this is the victory that has conquered and overcome the world—our [continuing, persistent] faith [in Jesus the Son of God].*

### ISAIAH 26:3 (AMPC)

*You will guard him and keep him in perfect and constant peace whose mind [both its inclination and its character] is stayed on You, because he commits himself to You, leans on You, and hopes confidently in You.*

## 2 CORINTHIANS 4:18 (KJV)

*While we look not at the things which are seen, but at the things which are not seen: for the things which are seen are temporal; but the things which are not seen are eternal.*

## PSALM 55:22 (AMPC)

*Cast your burden on the Lord [releasing the weight of it] and He will sustain you; He will never allow the [consistently] righteous to be moved (made to slip, fall, or fail).*

# GOD'S LOVE IS YOUR POWER TOOL

A power tool always makes the job easier. Ask someone who hammered nails all day how much faster they could work after the nail gun was invented. Not only did it speed up the process, but it took the strain out of the job.

Saving your loved one from destruction is God's idea. He wants to see them free even more than you want it. The rescue of your loved one doesn't have to drain all the spiritual energy out of your life because you can use God's power tools! You can pray from a heart established on and motivated by God's love.

God is ready and willing to intervene in the situation because He loves them. You must build confidence in His love. If you focus on what is seen, it will weaken your faith in God's love. For instance, when the person you are praying for is involved in drugs, alcohol, an eating disorder, or any other destructive lifestyle, you have physical evidence that tells you, "Your prayers aren't working!" Also, the situation might even make you think God is mad at your loved one because of their choices or lifestyle.

Building your faith in God's love will give you the greatest release of faith because His love motivates His salvation. Only the Word of God can transmit the accurate image of God's love. We tend to relate God's love for us based on experiences of how we have loved other people, but

GOD'S LOVE IS YOUR POWER TOOL

God's love for us surpasses any definition of love we can describe from human experience. His love is supernatural.

## CONNECT TO FAITH'S POWER SUPPLY!

You need a power supply of God's love to make your faith effective. Galatians 5:6 (KJV) says, "*For in Jesus Christ neither circumcision availeth any thing, nor uncircumcision; but faith which worketh by love.*"

You can have the greatest instrument, but without the power supply, it won't work. Unless it is plugged in, it will be inoperative. It must be connected to a power supply.

### GALATIANS 5:6 (WET)

*For in Christ Jesus neither circumcision is of any power nor uncircumcision, but faith coming to **effective** expression through love.*

Faith is one of the greatest spiritual tools God has given us. Yet, even if we have faith so great that we can move mountains, without love, it is empty (1 Cor. 13:2). Why? Faith works by love. When we build ourselves up praying in the Holy Spirit, we keep ourselves in God's love.

When we pray for loved ones, if we only operate in human motherly or fatherly love, it will reach a limit. Human love wears out and stretches thin. But the love of God shed abroad in our hearts by the Holy Ghost is a different type of love.

Let me explain. In the New Testament, there are different Greek words for love. There is *eros*, "romantic love," and *storge*, "familial love." There is

97

*phileo*, which is "friendship." But the New Testament word for *love* is a different word that specifically indicates God's love, which is vastly different from all those other types of love. First Corinthians 13 describes the love of God by illustrating how love thinks and behaves, even in adverse situations. Love is patient and kind. Love never takes account of a suffered wrong.

As a parent, I can say there have been times I ran short of my motherly love and needed God's love because I was put out with my children! They had plucked my last nerve and pushed me to the limit. I had to walk in the Spirit, so I would not fulfill the lust of my flesh!

The love of God that is shed abroad in our hearts by the Holy Spirit never wears out. First Corinthians 13:8 says that love never fails. That means it never grows thin. You can't pluck its last nerve. You can't push it to the end of the line where it says, "Okay! I am done. I can't love you anymore." No! God's love provides the spiritual energy to continue administering the intervention prayers until the answer comes.

## BELIEVING IN GOD'S LOVE

In our society, we have categories and definitions for love that mostly describe an emotion. But God's love is not an emotion! God is love, and this love can only be understood by God's Word. When we read the description of God's love in 1 Corinthians 13, we realize it doesn't operate like any other kind of love we have known.

### 1 CORINTHIANS 13:4-8 (WET)

*Love meekly and patiently bears ill treatment from others.*
*Love is kind, gentle, benign, pervading and penetrating the*

*whole nature, mellowing all which would have been harsh and austere; is not envious.*

*Love does not brag, nor does it show itself off, is not ostentatious, does not have an inflated ego, does not act unbecomingly, does not seek after the things which are its own, is not irritated, provoked, exasperated, aroused to anger, does not take into account the evil [which it suffers], does not rejoice at the iniquity but rejoices with the truth, endures all things, believes all things, hopes all things, bears up under all things, not losing heart nor courage. Love never fails.*

It will benefit your intervention prayers if you allow your definition of God's love to be the Bible's description of His love. Then, you will pray in light of how deeply He loves the person you are praying for.

Knowing and believing in the love of God is how we fellowship with God. We can pray this for our loved ones too!

## 1 JOHN 4:16 (KJV)

*And we have known and believed the love that God hath to us. God is love; and he that dwelleth in love dwelleth in God, and God in him.*

The believer who allows the Word of God to redefine God's love experiences God's love in a greater measure. We dwell in God, and God dwells in us. Imagine what a change it will make for our loved ones as they come to know His love. They will welcome God into their hearts!

The apostle Paul was inspired by the Holy Spirit to pray for the believers in Ephesus that they would be able to comprehend and know the love of Christ.

## EPHESIANS 3:17-19

*That Christ may dwell in your hearts through faith; that you, being rooted and grounded in love, may be able to comprehend with all the saints what is the width and length and depth and height—to know the love of Christ which passes knowledge; that you may be filled with all the fullness of God.*

According to this text, the key to being filled with the fullness of God is being rooted and grounded in love. We need a comprehension of the dimensions of the love of Christ. In other words, we need to know how deeply He loves us and understand how far His love for us will reach.

Adversity is designed to make us crumble or sink like Peter began to sink when he turned his attention to the problem. But God's love is designed to be the foundation of our faith. When we know and believe that God's love is abounding to us, we will become unmovable.

## ROMANS 8:37

*Yet in all these things we are more than conquerors through Him who loved us.*

Nothing can separate us from this love that makes us more than conquerors. No struggle, weapon, or problem can defeat us as we learn to live in this love. So, let's ask God to open our spiritual eyes and show us how deeply He loves us. Let's ask Him to show us how much He loves the people we are targeting with our prayers.

God wants to free our loved ones and establish their lives in His plan. He cares about their future and wants to demonstrate His love in the present situation.

# LOOKING AT GOD'S LOVE

## 2 CORINTHIANS 4:18 (KJV)

*While we look not at the things which are seen, but at the things which are not seen: for the things which are seen are temporal; but the things which are not seen are eternal.*

Remember, the word *temporal* means "subject to change." The things that are visible to the natural eye are subject to change. This includes addiction, depression, criminal activity, suicide attempts, etc. What you see happening in his or her life is subject to change. We are not supposed to focus our attention on these temporary things. Yet, God's eternal love won't change. When we focus our attention on the eternal truth of God's love, God's glory is at work in the situation.

## PSALM 27:13

*I would have lost heart, unless I had believed that I would see the goodness of the Lord in the land of the living.*

Moses asked to see the glory of God, but God showed Him His goodness. In God's definition, His goodness is His glory!

## EXODUS 33:18-19

*And he said, "Please, show me Your glory."*
*Then He said, "I will make all My goodness pass before you,*

When God descended to reveal His glory, He proclaimed His mercy and spoke of His goodness.

## EXODUS 34:5-6 (AMPC)

*And the Lord descended in the cloud and stood with him there and proclaimed the name of the Lord.*

*And the Lord passed by before him, and proclaimed, The Lord! the Lord! a God merciful and gracious, slow to anger, and abundant in loving-kindness and truth.*

The word *merciful* means "to love deeply, to have mercy, to have tender affection, to be full of compassion." The word *gracious* means "to show favor, to be inclined toward or to extend favor or grace." As we take God's description of Himself and know Him by His Word, we develop our trust in Him.

## JOHN 3:16 (AMPC)

*For God so **greatly loved and dearly prized** the world that He [even] gave up His only begotten (unique) Son, so that whoever believes in (trusts in, clings to, relies on) Him shall not perish (come to destruction, be lost) but have eternal (everlasting) life.*

Our Heavenly Father greatly loves and dearly prizes our loved ones so much that He sent Jesus to provide a way for them to escape destruction. The way has been made! Salvation is ready!

So, let's focus on His goodness and give it more attention than any of the issues that try to make us doubt. God's goodness will not change!

# YOUR INTERVENTION PRAYER

According to Ephesians 3:17-19, Heavenly Father, I ask that Christ settle down in my heart through faith, that I would be firmly rooted and grounded in love. Let Your love become the motivation of my faith and the boldness of my petition.

Help me see *(insert your loved one's name)* through Your love. Help me to have compassion and mercy on their failures and poor decisions. I forgive them for anything they have done to me and the injury they may have caused our family.

I ask that I would be able to grasp the breadth, width, height, and depth of Your love and that I would experience this love in a greater way so I can pray for *(insert your loved one's name)* in that flow of love.

In Jesus' name, I pray that You would reveal these dimensions of Your love to *(insert your loved one's name)* and lead them to experience Your love too. Lord, I ask that *(insert your loved one's name)* would know and believe the love You have for him/her. Let that love drive out any hopelessness they may feel. I surround *(insert your loved one's name)* with faith and love like a protective shield.

Father God, I choose to focus on Your love for *(insert your loved one's name)* and speak in line with Your truth about the condition of his/her life. I stand in faith that You love *(insert your loved one's name)* even more than I love him/her.

Thank You, Lord, for loving *(insert your loved one's name)*. Thank You, Lord, for drawing him/her by Your Spirit. I rejoice and praise You for releasing Your love into *(insert your loved one's name)'s* life.

# BUILD YOUR FAITH

## JOHN 3:16-17 (MSG)

*This is how much God loved the world: He gave his Son, his one and only Son. And this is why: so that no one need be destroyed; by believing in him, anyone can have a whole and lasting life. God didn't go to all the trouble of sending his Son merely to point an accusing finger, telling the world how bad it was. He came to help, to put the world right again.*

## PSALM 27:13 (MSG)

*I'm sure now I'll see God's goodness in the exuberant earth. Stay with God! Take heart. Don't quit. I'll say it again: Stay with God.*

## PSALM 86:15 (KJV)

*But thou, O Lord, art a God full of compassion, and gracious, long suffering, and plenteous in mercy and truth.*

## PSALM 145:8-9 (KJV)

*The Lord is gracious, and full of compassion; slow to anger, and of great mercy. The Lord is good to all: and his tender mercies are over all his works.*

# DAY 12

# YOUR HOTLINE TO HEAVEN

As established in previous chapters, the basis of your intervention prayer is the will of God. You locate the will of God in the Word of God. By using the Word to develop an image of God's will in your heart, you develop confidence before you pray.

Next, your intervention prayer needs the proper focus. In the past, I have wasted precious time praying with the wrong focus, so I want to help you identify the objective to ensure yours is correct.

Let's rule out some of the *wrong* things people target in prayer. First, we are *not* praying to convince God or talk Him into doing something He does not want to do. Instead, we are partnering with Him in prayer, using our faith and authority to pray His will. We are allowing our faith-filled prayers to work like an instrument in the hand of God.

Second, we are *not* trying to tell God the problem. He knows every detail of every situation in every person's life. Nothing we can say will catch the Lord off guard! Therefore, we don't need to spend most of our time in prayer rehearsing the sordid details or describing the desperate situation. Instead, our prayers should be filled with rehearsing the spiritual answers and promises of God.

Finally, we are not trying to get God to save our loved ones. He has already made every provision for their salvation. When they make the decision to *accept* His salvation in Jesus Christ, they will be born again and set free from every bondage. So, our prayers focus on helping our loved ones see and accept the love, deliverance, and salvation God has provided in Jesus Christ.

# CONNECT AND DISCONNECT

In a simple explanation, our focus is to connect and disconnect. We want to connect them to the power and ability of God and disconnect them from the authority and influence of the adversary.

Let me explain the dilemma. God has given people the free will to choose their destiny. In addition, God gave mankind the authority to dominate the earth. So, there are a lot of things that happen because of someone's bad decision or their failure to exercise dominion. Due to a lack of knowledge about these two truths, people blame God for many things that He has placed into someone else's jurisdiction.

The problem arises when we misunderstand the word *sovereign,* which means "all reign" or "all rule." God is indeed all-powerful and sovereign, but He delegated the authority of the earth to mankind.

### GENESIS 1:26-28

*Then God said, "Let Us make man in Our image, according to Our likeness; let them have dominion over the fish of the sea, over the birds of the air, and over the cattle, over all the earth and over every creeping thing that creeps on the earth." So God created man in His own image; in the image of God He created him; male and female He created them. Then God blessed them, and God said to them, "Be fruitful and multiply; fill the*

*earth and subdue it; have dominion over the fish of the sea, over the birds of the air, and over every living thing that moves on the earth."*

God established mankind as His representative. Originally, God covered us in His glory as part of the equipment to represent Him. The phrase *crowned with glory* means "heavy, weighty, one who carries a lot of weight."

## PSALM 8:3-8 (AMPC)

*When I view and consider Your heavens, the work of Your fingers, the moon and the stars, which You have ordained and established, what is man that You are mindful of him, and the son of [earthborn] man that You care for him? Yet You have made him but a little lower than God [or heavenly beings], and You have crowned him with glory and honor. You made him to have dominion over the works of Your hands; You have put all things under his feet: all sheep and oxen, yes, and the beasts of the field, the birds of the air, and the fish of the sea, and whatever passes along the paths of the seas.*

Since God delegated the authority on the earth to mankind, there are many things He is no longer overseeing. He expects us to put things in order according to what we find in His Word. We are responsible for enforcing the will of God and resisting the devil.

God gave us free will. Every human being can choose God's will or disregard it. If we choose His ways, we will have God's results—His blessing, protection, wisdom, etc. But the Lord won't override our decision when we go our own way. God will respectfully stay on the outside, looking in and waiting until we invite Him to help us.

That is where our prayers come into play. When our loved ones disregard God's will, we can ask the Lord to intervene. Because of our prayers, God has a legal right to "knock on the door of their hearts." He has the legal access to show them things, speak to their hearts, or send laborers across their paths.

## A DIRECT LINE OF COMMUNICATION

I grew up watching reruns of the 1960s *Batman* series starring Adam West. In this show, the mayor of Gotham City had a red phone on his desk that was a direct telephone line to Batman's cave or even the Batmobile. The mayor had instant access to the help of the "caped crusader."

But you have a direct line of communication with the Creator of the Universe! You don't have to schedule an appointment, go through a background check, or be patted down by security to have a meeting with Him. Instead, you can go straight to God and receive help in times of need.

### HEBREWS 4:16 (KJV)

*Let us therefore come boldly unto the throne of grace, that we may obtain mercy, and find grace to help in time of need.*

The Amplified Bible, Classic Edition, says, *"Let us then fearlessly and confidently and boldly draw near."* Our confidence is in the fact that God hears us, and He will answer. Do you have this level of confidence?

In my experience serving in the local church for more than 25 years, I have found that many Christians don't have much confidence in their prayers. They ask the pastor, leaders in the church, or a ministry with a call center that is offering prayer to do their praying for them.

This is not God's design! James 5:13 (AMPC) says, *"Is anyone among you afflicted (ill-treated, suffering evil)? He should pray."* While having believers who agree with us in prayer is an added benefit, it is not wise to leave our praying to others. For instance, I can ask you to pray for my child, but you won't pray from the same position of authority or with the same supplication that I will use. You can pray a general prayer for God to help or save, but you probably won't think about it tomorrow or the next day.

We need to develop confidence that God Himself hears us when we pray. According to Scripture, that confidence will be followed with an assurance that He will answer.

## 1 JOHN 5:14-15 (AMPC)

*And this is the confidence (the assurance, the privilege of boldness) which we have in Him: [we are sure] that if we ask anything (make any request) according to His will (in agreement with His own plan), He listens to and hears us.*

*And if (since) we [positively] know that He listens to us in whatever we ask, **we also know [with settled and absolute knowledge]** that we have [granted us as our present possessions] the requests made of Him.*

This text says, *"we also know [with settled and absolute knowledge] that we have...the requests."* When do we have it? The answers begin moving toward the situation as soon as we pray. Like the first responders who are dispatched as soon as the call is made to 911, God's help is "en route."

We may not see what God is doing behind the scenes, but we know with settled and absolute knowledge God is moving on our behalf.

## DANIEL 9:3-4 (KJV)

*And I set my face unto the Lord God, to seek by prayer and supplications, with fasting, and sackcloth, and ashes: and I prayed unto the Lord my God.*

Daniel set himself to pray about things in his nation, praying for people and situations around him to get in line with God's plan. When the angel arrived with an answer, the angel said, *"At the beginning of thy supplications the commandment came forth, and I am come to shew thee"* (Dan. 9:23 KJV). The answer began moving from the moment Daniel prayed!

In the next chapter, we see that Daniel was in another focused time of praying and seeking God. An angel came in response to Daniel's prayer and said, *"Fear not, Daniel: for from the first day that thou didst set thine heart to understand, and to chasten thyself before thy God, thy words were heard, and I am come for thy words"* (Dan. 10:12 KJV). If Daniel received immediate action in response to his prayers under a lesser covenant, how much more shall we, under *"a better covenant...established upon better promises"* (Heb. 8:6 KJV), receive immediate action when we pray?

When you pick up your prayer hotline to your Heavenly Father, He is receiving your call. You have a direct line of communication!

# YOUR INTERVENTION PRAYER

In the name of Jesus, I come boldly today to pray about situations in the life of *(insert your loved one's name)*. Father, I believe that You hear me and respond immediately to begin working in this situation. Lord, You even show me things to pray and ways to intercede for *(insert your loved one's name)*. I trust in You.

I am releasing my faith for *(insert your loved one's name)* to know this love and receive the sacrifice Jesus has made for him/her. Father God, I ask You to help *(insert your loved one's name)* to see and comprehend Your love. Open the eyes of his/her understanding so that he/she may see your salvation in Christ Jesus. I break Satan's mind-blinding control over their thoughts and declare *(insert your loved one's name)* to be free in Jesus' name.

Thank You that I have a direct line of communication to reach You. You are a very present and well-proved help in a time of trouble (Ps. 46:1 AMPC).

Heavenly Father, I pray from Deuteronomy 30:6 that You would circumcise the heart of *(insert your loved one's name)* to love You. Let Your glory appear to *(insert your loved one's name)* (Ps. 90:6).

John 6:44 says, *"No one can come to Me unless the Father who sent Me draws him."* Heavenly Father, I ask You to draw (insert your loved one's name). Deal with their heart. Reveal Your goodness to (insert your loved one's name), in Jesus' name.

# BUILD YOUR FAITH

### HEBREWS 10:22 (WET)

*Let us keep on drawing near with a genuinely true heart in full assurance of faith, having had our hearts sprinkled from an evil conscience and having had our body washed with pure water.*

### JOHN 15:7-8

*If you abide in Me, and My words abide in you, you will ask what you desire, and it shall be done for you. By this My Father is glorified, that you bear much fruit; so you will be My disciples.*

### JOHN 15:7-8 (WET)

*If you maintain a living communion with me and my words are at home in you, I command you to ask, at once, something for yourself, whatever your heart desires, and it will become yours. In this my Father is glorified, namely, that you are bearing much fruit. So shall you become my disciples.*

### MATTHEW 7:7-8

*Ask, and it will be given to you; seek, and you will find; knock, and it will be opened to you. For everyone who asks receives, and he who seeks finds, and to him who knocks it will be opened.*

# STOCK THE SHELVES WITH GOD'S ANSWERS

Faith-filled prayers make wisdom, strength, and power available for our loved ones to access. I like to think of our intervention prayers as "stocking shelves." We are stocking the spiritual shelves so that as they need help, hope, and answers, they can reach up on the shelf and find a spiritual supply, see the light, and have access to salvation available to them.

## JAMES 5:16 (AMPC)

*The earnest (heartfelt, continued) prayer of a righteous man* **makes tremendous power available** *[dynamic in its working].*

The prayers we pray from our position as righteous believers in Christ Jesus are prayers that are full of power and effective. Our prayers are accomplishing things. Prayer makes tremendous power available!

One day, I stopped by the store to pick up some needed items right before the store closed for the night. I expected to find an empty store with employees who were ready to lock the doors, turn off the lights, and go home. Instead, I found employees just starting their shifts, pulling out boxes and crates. They were ready to spend the next eight hours stocking the shelves for the following business day.

The workers were busy taking inventory. They assessed the situation to discover what shelves had been emptied and what was on hand to refill that area. They didn't wait until their reserves were empty, either. Instead, they placed an order to replenish the stock so they would not run out. Keeping the shelves abundantly supplied was their focus!

That is what you are doing in the spirit realm! You are taking inventory, ordering supplies and stocking the shelves! You can surround your loved one with a supply of wisdom, answers, and insight so that when they begin to seek, they shall readily find. Your prayers provide spiritual flows of protection, love, and faith around their lives so that, while they are in the valley of decision, they have God's power drawing them in the right direction. God is able to use the power released in your prayers to turn the situation and influence the one you are praying for.

## PHILIPPIANS 1:19 (AMPC)

*For I am well assured and indeed know **that through your prayers** and a bountiful supply of the Spirit of Jesus Christ (the Messiah) this will turn out for my preservation (for the spiritual health and welfare of my own soul) and avail toward the saving work of the Gospel.*

When you see the phrase *"a bountiful supply of the Spirit of Jesus Christ,"* you may be tempted to disregard what the Scripture says before it. The phrase *"through your prayers"* identifies a primary ingredient in Paul's preservation and the turnaround he needed. In the case of your loved ones, it is often your prayers that open up the supply of the Spirit. You are the one walking through the aisles, inspecting the empty shelves and placing the order for what is needed.

Ask yourself this question: What would happen if I didn't pray? How much access would God have to this situation if no one asked Him for help? Without an invitation, there is a limit to how much God will intervene in the lives of human beings.

Think about the Shunammite woman who went to get the help of Elisha in 2 Kings 4. She was the one who brought the power of God that turned her son's life around. Yes, Elisha administered the power. But it was the boy's mother who brought God's power into the situation. She placed a demand on the supply chain, and God delivered supernatural power to stock the shelves with what she needed. The boy needed the power, but he couldn't call for it. The Shunammite woman made the call. She prayed the intervention prayer.

## JESUS STOCKED PETER'S SHELVES

### LUKE 22:31-32

*And the Lord said, "Simon, Simon! Indeed, Satan has asked for you, that he may sift you as wheat. **But I have prayed for you, that your faith should not fail;** and when you have returned to Me, strengthen your brethren."*

Jesus provided a spiritual supply that Peter didn't even know he would need. The Lord prayed an intervention prayer that equipped Peter in advance of the difficulty. Jesus is your example. There are things the enemy is planning against your loved ones, but your prayers will provide the light and mercy they need to overcome it.

115

When I was living in sin, bound by addiction, I would have never thought of asking God to help me because I thought God hated me. I didn't expect Him to be interested in my life. God only had access to me through the people who loved me. My grandma, my mother, and my children prayed for me. My children even asked their Sunday school teachers to pray for me. Their prayers provided a legal right for God to approach me and opened an avenue for God to draw me to Him.

Never underestimate the power that is being produced when you pray. Your prayers are stocking the shelves, making tremendous power available!

## YOUR INTERVENTION PRAYER

Father, I approach You in the name of my Savior, Jesus Christ. I am praying for *(insert your loved one's name)* who needs to know Your love. I pray that You would surround *(insert your loved one's name)* with a supply of truth. Psalm 25:10 says, "*All the paths of the Lord are mercy and truth*," and John 1:17 declares, "*grace and truth came through Jesus Christ*." Let Your paths lead him/her to the truth in Jesus Christ.

Lord, surround *(insert your loved one's name)* with wisdom. Jesus is made unto us wisdom (1 Cor. 1:30). When they roam, let wisdom lead them. When they sleep, let wisdom keep them. When they awake, let wisdom speak to them (Prov. 6:22).

According to Psalm 51:12, restore joy to *(insert your loved one's name)* and uphold them with a willing spirit. I call on Your promise in Jeremiah

30:17, which says You will restore us to health and heal our wounds. Lord, You promised in Ezekiel 34:16 that You will seek the lost and bring back the strays. You will bind up the injured and strengthen the weak. I ask You to do these things for *(insert your loved one's name)*.

I ask You to send laborers to *(insert your loved one's name)* that he/she will receive from. Send people who can relate to him/her and strengthen those people with boldness and the anointing to share Your gospel to *(insert your loved one's name)*. I praise You for Your goodness! I praise You for Your faithfulness to Your Word.

## BUILD YOUR FAITH

### 1 CORINTHIANS 16:13 (WET)

*Be keeping a watchful eye ever open. Be standing fast in the faith. Be showing yourselves to be men. Be mighty in strength.*

### MATTHEW 21:22 (KJV)

*And all things, whatsoever ye shall ask in prayer, believing, ye shall receive.*

## 1 THESSALONIANS 5:4-6 (AMPC)

*But you are not in [given up to the power of] darkness, brethren, for that day to overtake you by surprise like a thief. For you are all sons of light and sons of the day; we do not belong either to the night or to darkness. Accordingly then, let us not sleep, as the rest do, but let us keep wide awake (alert, watchful, cautious, and on our guard) and let us be sober (calm, collected, and circumspect).*

# THORNS
# IN THE ROAD

Lisa stood before me in the prayer line, asking me to agree in prayer for her son's deliverance from an addiction to meth. After hearing how the Lord had changed my life, her hope was strengthened that things could change for her son.

His parents raised him in church, but when he entered his teenage years, he turned his back on God, claiming to hate Him. What began with wild partying, drinking, and getting high escalated until their son, deeply entrenched in a gang running a meth lab, was targeted in an undercover sting.

I had the privilege of celebrating with them when their son came back to the Lord. It was a process of restoration that included an arrest, a short time in rehab, and a sincere desire on his part to make a change in his life.

But his father told me a specific verse that the Lord led him to pray during that time. It was such a useful tool that I want to share it with you. It is a verse that speaks of Hosea's wayward wife, Gomer.

### HOSEA 2:6

*Therefore, behold, I will hedge up your way with thorns, and wall her in, so that she cannot find her paths.*

My friend took this verse and began asking God to "hedge up" or block his son's path. Isn't this what we need when we see our loved ones taking paths that could ruin their lives, destroy their marriages, or end in death? What a thing to pray!

God's Word Translation reads, *"That is why I will block her way with thornbushes and build a wall so that she can't get through."*

The Bible in Basic English says, *"For this cause I will put thorns in her road, building up a wall round her so that she may not go on her way."*

The Passion Translation says, *"But I'll block her way with a thorn hedge; I'll put a wall up around her, blocking her usual paths."*

As this father prayed for God to block his son's paths, the Lord began to intervene. He ended up in police custody, reached a point of decision, and yielded to God. The Lord restored his life! He is a valuable part of our church today, serving God and leading his family in the Word.

Let's be clear that we are not talking about the old religious idea that says, "God will wrap them around a telephone pole to get their attention." *No!* That is what the devil wants. He comes to steal, kill, and destroy. On the contrary, we invite God to thwart the *enemy's plans* and stop our loved ones from continuing on the path that would destroy them.

At one point, the Lord prompted me to pray, "Father, don't let my children get away with lies and deception. Whatever is done in the dark, let it come to the light. Lord, bring anything they have hidden from us to the light so we can teach them to walk in truth."

## LUKE 12:3 (AMPC)

*Whatever you have spoken in the darkness shall be heard and listened to in the light, and what you have whispered in*

*[people's] ears and behind closed doors will be proclaimed upon the housetops.*

At the time, I didn't have any indication that they had lied about anything. I simply had a prompting to pray along those lines. Soon, my prayer began to bring out areas of deception. I found a hiding place in the attic opening at the top of a closet where one of my teenagers had hidden alcohol. That was just the beginning.

The light began to shine on the things they were doing in secret. I was shocked! At one point, the police and school organized a sting to break up the secret fight club my son had started! He had to break the news to me before I saw him on the evening news!

Another situation occurred one Sunday evening. I ended the final song in the song service and transitioned the service to my husband. As I walked down the aisle of the church, headed to the water fountain, the Lord spoke clearly to my heart, "Go home *now!*"

One of my children, claiming to be sick, had stayed home from church. I went straight to my car and drove home. As I neared my home, I saw a car in my driveway that I didn't recognize. I walked in the door just in time to confront an adult who connected with my teenager over the internet. I arrived just in time. Thank God!

The Lord was faithful in showing me how to pray and when to act. The things that came to light shocked me but taught my children that deception would never profit. God was blocking their way to stop them from traveling a path of deceit.

God knows what is needed to break through the unbelief and how to reveal His goodness in a way our loved ones will comprehend. Let's pray with the promptings and leadings of the Spirit of God.

# YOUR INTERVENTION PRAYER

Father God, I come to You in the name of Jesus on behalf of *(insert your loved one's name)*. The god of this world has tried to blind his/her mind from seeing Your love. According to Luke 10:19, I have authority over the power of the enemy, so I break his influence over *(insert your loved one's name)*. I command that *(insert your loved one's name)* be free from all bondage so that he/she can understand God's plan for his/her life.

Father, I ask You to hedge up every evil path that *(insert your loved one's name)* is walking. Build a wall in the road of destruction to block *(insert your loved one's name)* from continuing down that road. Protect them from the influences of evil people and hinder the plans of Satan on every hand.

In the name of Jesus, I ask You to bring to the light the things being done in the darkness. Let *(insert your loved one's name)* understand that lies and deception are playing a part in his/her destruction. Strengthen *(insert your loved one's name)* to embrace Your Word as truth. Give *(insert your loved one's name)* a desire to walk in the light.

According to Psalm 16:11, show *(insert your loved one's name)* the path of life and let him/her find the fullness of joy in your presence. Hold up *(insert your loved one's name)*'s goings in Your path that his/her footsteps do not slip (Ps. 17:5). All of your paths are mercy and truth, so teach *(insert your loved one's name)* Your paths (Ps. 25:10,4). Thank You, Heavenly Father, for Your help. I worship You!

# BUILD YOUR FAITH

## DEUTERONOMY 7:9 (KJV)

*Know therefore that the Lord thy God, he is God, the faithful God, which keepeth covenant and mercy with them that love him and keep his commandments to a thousand generations.*

## PSALM 36:5

*Your mercy, O Lord, is in the heavens; Your faithfulness reaches to the clouds.*

## PSALM 86:15

*But You, O Lord, are a God full of compassion, and gracious, longsuffering and abundant in mercy and truth.*

## PSALM 36:7

*How excellent is thy lovingkindness, O God! Therefore the children of men put their trust under the shadow of thy wings.*

# WEEK THREE

## INTERVENTION STORY:

# RESCUED
# BY PRAYER

Philip was running as hard and fast as he could from God and the call God had placed on his life. It wasn't easy, though. In the small town of Dalhart, Texas, everyone knew him as the preacher's kid. His parents had pastored there long enough that even though they had returned to the evangelistic field, traveling and preaching across the United States, the people around town still identified Philip as the pastor's son. When he was singing or playing drums in the bar, people would ask things like, "Aren't you the son of the preacher?" or "Didn't you used to preach in the youth group?" or "Weren't you the drummer at the church down the street?" He worked hard to tear down that "church kid" image that everyone had of him.

Alcohol controlled Philip's decisions, leading him into the bar every payday and holding him there until all his money was gone. He journeyed from couch to couch, bumming off his friends until he overstayed his welcome. At one point, he found shelter by sneaking into someone's garage and hiding away until morning. It was a bleak, lonely time in his life.

But things grew worse when Philip made some enemies in town. He thought he was arriving at a party, but instead, it was an ambush. Philip found himself face to face with two brawny men and one scorned woman armed with bats, ready to beat him to a pulp. Knowing he was outnumbered, Philip took off running, sprinting through a field. The threats and taunts of the men were drowned out by the sound of their pickup truck as they gunned the engine to catch up to him. Gasping for breath, he realized he couldn't outrun them.

They stepped out of the truck and surrounded him. As the beating began, Philip was knocked to the ground. The thud of a steel-toed boot cracked against his skull, causing his ears to ring and his head to swim. His back, his ribs, and his head took the brunt of this brutal beating as

Philip gave up trying to fight against his three assailants and tried to cover his head. Blow after blow met their mark until Philip realized, "I'm going to die right here in this field."

But Philip's parents knew how to call for God's intervention. His parents knew the path Philip had been walking. They knew about the alcohol, the bars, and the homelessness. When his mom saw him, she would say, "You know God has a plan for your life." His dad tried the authoritative approach, saying, "You'd better get things right, boy!" Even though their attempts to convince Philip to return to God's paths weren't working, their prayers made God's power available.

That is what happened on this night. His mother was awakened from her sleep with a strong urgency to pray for her son. As she got out of bed and began to cry out for Philip, the Lord spoke to her, "The devil is trying to kill your son." She took her place of authority and bound the enemy's plan. She declared her son would not die but live and declare the works of the Lord (Ps. 118:17). She prayed until she sensed the peace of God and then went back to bed.

In the field, the beating stopped. Without a word, the three assailants stopped their frenzied attack and walked back to their truck. They drove off, and Philip found himself alone and alive.

He managed to drag his battered and broken body out of the field and make his way to the county hospital. He wondered how he had survived and what made his attackers stop until he spoke to his mother later that day. When they compared the hour of her praying to the hour of his assault, it was the same. His mother reached God's 911 operator, and God's power was sent to the scene.

He turned back to God, and the Lord restored his life and put him back on track to His plan. Today, Philip Steele is my husband. For over

126

25 years, he has pastored Faith Builders International Church and Fellowship. But Philip is aware of the difference his mother's prayer made in providing God legal access to help him in his time of need.

# DAY 15

# HOW TO
# PRACTICE VICTORY

Your intervention prayers are tools to initiate the plan of God in your loved one's life. You need to know the tools in your toolbox and how to use them with skill. Remember this: You don't want to limit yourself to your favorite type of praying, which could hinder your effectiveness. You want to use the right tool to get the job done right.

Sometimes, I use a butter knife to drive a nail in the wall or tighten a screw. My husband shakes his head and chuckles as he goes to the garage, digs around in his toolbox, and returns with the right tool for the job. With the right tool, the task is always easier *and* more effective.

Many people think they can fix *everything* with the prayer of faith. The prayer of faith (often referred to as *the prayer of petition*) is used to receive the promises of God that belong to us in our covenant. The Scripture provides the faith or basis of our belief that God has given us that provision. With the prayer of faith or petition, we ask for it, believing that we receive it (Mark 11:23-24).

While the prayer of faith may be the type of prayer we use more often, it is not always the most effective in every situation. When praying for our loved ones, their will is involved, and the Lord won't allow us to use *our* faith against *their* will. So, we need to know which tool to use and how to use it. If we need to cut a board, it would be frustrating to use a drill. A saw would work better! If we need to intercede, let's reach for the intercession tool. If we need to supplicate, let's reach for our supplications.

## PREPARE THE ATMOSPHERE

One tool in the intervention toolbox is the prayer of praise and worship. This is also referred to in Scripture as "ministering to the Lord."

### ACTS 13:1-4 (KJV)

*Now there were in the church that was at Antioch certain prophets and teachers; as Barnabas, and Simeon that was called Niger, and Lucius of Cyrene, and Manaen, which had been brought up with Herod the tetrarch, and Saul. **As they ministered to the Lord**, and fasted, the Holy Ghost said, Separate me Barnabas and Saul for the work whereunto I have called them. And when they had fasted and prayed, and laid their hands on them, they sent them away. So they, being sent forth by the Holy Ghost, departed unto Seleucia; and from thence they sailed to Cyprus.*

The phrase "as they ministered to the Lord" reveals the motive of their activity. In their worship and reverence of the Lord, they prepared an atmosphere where the Lord could speak clearly about the direction of their lives and ministry. They received details and specific direction as they ministered to the Lord in an atmosphere where God was exalted. The Lord had their attention and showed them the next step.

We must minister to the Lord! As we do, we open the way for God to move in our situation and reveal the direction He wants us to take. We fix our attention on Him and make it easy for Him to show us things.

When we minister to the Lord, we give Him our focus and turn away from the trouble.

### ACTS 16:25-26 (KJV)

*And at midnight Paul and Silas prayed, and sang praises unto God: and the prisoners heard them. And suddenly there was a great earthquake, so that the foundations of the prison were shaken: and immediately all the doors were opened, and every one's bands were loosed.*

While "midnight" refers to a specific time, it can also refer to a season in our lives. Paul and Silas were beaten and persecuted for setting someone free. They were thrust into prison, and their feet were in stocks. I'm sure their situation was difficult on their mind and emotions. But as Paul and Silas prayed and sang praises to God, the power of God manifested.

When you are dealing with a situation with your loved one that is out of your control, you can worship the Lord. You can create an atmosphere where God is exalted above the problem. When you praise His name, there is a manifestation of His presence in the atmosphere around you and a greater manifestation of His ability to break the limitations and strongholds.

The Bible says those who wait upon the Lord shall renew their strength (Isa. 40:31). To *wait* doesn't mean "waiting idly." Instead, it means "to wait upon the Lord and minister to Him." Talk about how good and faithful God is! Proclaim that God is faithful to His Word. He is a cove-nant-keeping God!

Ministering to the Lord is strength for you, so develop a lifestyle of praise. You can glorify God in advance for the freedom and salvation of your family members.

## YOUR INTERVENTION PRAYER

Father, I approach Your throne in Jesus' name. I know Your will for *(insert your loved one's name)* is liberty, freedom, and a life of wholeness. I pray for *(insert your loved one's name)* to be free from the fear of approach-ing You. I pray that he/she would come to know that Jesus has provided an approach to You through the blood He poured out on the cross at Calvary.

Father, I resist the opportunity to feel sorry for myself. I recognize the pressure of the enemy to make me think like a victim, and I refuse to participate. I plead the blood of Jesus to cleanse my mind and emotions from thoughts of self-pity, shame, or embarrassment. With the weapons of my warfare, I cast down imaginations that cause me to see myself as the victim.

Instead, I rejoice in Your faithfulness. I lift my voice to say, "Thank You for giving me Your Word as a light to live by." I stir myself to praise You in advance for the laborers whom You will send across *(insert your loved one's name)*'s path. I rejoice that You are faithful to draw *(insert your loved one's name)* by Your Spirit.

I pray for *(insert your loved one's name)* to hear Your voice and Your Word. I pray for *(insert your loved one's name)* to understand the plan of salvation and turn in Your direction.

## BUILD YOUR FAITH

### PSALM 103:1-5 (KJV)

*Bless the Lord, O my soul: and all that is within me, bless his holy name. Bless the Lord, O my soul, and forget not all his benefits: who forgiveth all thine iniquities; who healeth all thy diseases; who redeemeth thy life from destruction; who crowneth thee with lovingkindness and tender mercies; who satisfieth thy mouth with good things; so that thy youth is renewed like the eagle's.*

### JEREMIAH 31:16-17 (AMPC)

*Thus says the Lord: Restrain your voice from weeping and your eyes from tears, for your work shall be rewarded, says the Lord;* and **[your children] shall return from the enemy's land.** *And there is hope for your future, says the Lord;* **your children shall come back** *to their own country.*

# IT IS VICTORY— NOT VICTIM

I spent many years practicing being a victim. I blamed everyone else for my situation and felt sorry for myself when things were hard. I rehearsed the times that people had rejected or mistreated me. The victim mentality became a way of life. But after I accepted Jesus as Lord, it didn't fit me anymore because, in Christ, I am more than a conqueror (Rom. 8:27). I have the victory that overcomes the world (1 John 5:4), and God always causes me to triumph (2 Cor. 2:14).

A *victim* is "one who is harmed or made to suffer from a circumstance or event." On the other hand, a *victor* is "one who defeats an adversary, the winner in a fight, battle, or contest." We are victors in every situation because of our position in Christ Jesus.

## 1 CORINTHIANS 15:57 (KJV)

*But thanks be to God, which giveth us the victory through our Lord Jesus Christ.*

Remember and rehearse your victory when situations with your loved one cause turmoil and chaos in your family. When things happen that make you feel like a victim, choose to stay in victory. Resist the temptation to feel sorry for yourself. You must overcome the shame caused by the poor decisions your loved one makes because the enemy uses those feelings to move you out of the flow of love and faith. You must maintain the triumph you have in Christ.

For example, King Jehoshaphat and the people of Judah maintained their victory and received God's help. They were under attack and outnumbered. They could have felt sorry for themselves or taken the victim's position. Instead, they sought God.

## 2 CHRONICLES 20:1-4

*It happened after this that the people of Moab with the people of Ammon, and others with them besides the Ammonites, came to battle against Jehoshaphat. Then some came and told Jehoshaphat, saying, "A great multitude is coming against you from beyond the sea, from Syria; and they are in Hazazon Tamar" (which is En Gedi). And Jehoshaphat feared, and set himself to seek the Lord, and proclaimed a fast throughout all Judah. So Judah gathered together to ask help from the Lord; and from all the cities of Judah they came to seek the Lord.*

When King Jehoshaphat prayed, he prayed from the position of victory. His focus was on God's might, provision, and faithfulness. Look specifically at the emphasis of his prayer.

## 2 CHRONICLES 20:5-9

*Then Jehoshaphat stood in the assembly of Judah and Jerusalem, in the house of the Lord, before the new court, and said: "O Lord God of our fathers, **are You not God in heaven**, and **do You not rule over all** the kingdoms of the nations, and **in Your hand is there not power and might**, so that **no one is able to withstand You?***

*"Are **You** not our God, who **drove out the inhabitants** of this land before Your people Israel, and **gave it to the descendants of Abraham** Your friend forever? And they dwell in it, and have built You a sanctuary in it for Your name, saying, 'If disaster comes upon us—sword, judgment, pestilence, or famine—we will stand before this temple and in Your presence (for Your name is in this temple), and cry out to You in our affliction, and You will hear and save.'"*

The king prayed with an emphasis on God's goodness, His might, and past victories. Jehoshaphat established that God gave them the land and would help them keep it.

## 2 CHRONICLES 20:10-12

*And now, here are the people of Ammon, Moab, and Mount Seir—whom You would not let Israel invade when they came out of the land of Egypt, but they turned from them and did not destroy them—here they are, rewarding us by coming to throw us out of Your possession which You have given us to inherit. O our God, will You not judge them? For we have no power against this great multitude that is coming against us; nor do we know what to do, but **our eyes are upon You.***

Now that we have studied Jehoshaphat's approach to God in prayer, let's see God's response. The Spirit of God came on a prophet, saying, *"Thus says the Lord to you: 'Do not be afraid nor dismayed because of this great multitude, for the battle is not yours, but God's...You will not need to fight in this battle. Position yourselves, stand still and see the salvation of the Lord, who is with you, O Judah and Jerusalem!' Do not fear or be dismayed; tomorrow go out against them, for the Lord is with you"* (2 Chron. 20:15-17).

135

They believed God's declaration so completely that they didn't send the armed men out to the front lines. Instead, they sent the singers out in front to battle. When the praise and thanksgiving started, God defeated the adversary. The victory established in the king's prayer came into manifestation as they praised the Lord.

Giving God thanks is the easiest way to get into the flow of faith and stay in faith. You can come out of any situation when you take God at His Word and begin to say "thank you" in advance. Your thanksgiving is proof that you believe you have received before you see any evidence in the natural circumstance.

## PRAISE IS STRENGTH

When you are in a situation, standing for a loved one, you must recognize praise and worship as a tool and a weapon. God's strength is available in our praise. When we begin to praise God, His strength and ability come on the scene.

### PSALM 8:2

*Out of the mouth of babes and nursing infants You have ordained strength, because of Your enemies, that You may silence the enemy and the avenger.*

Jesus testified that *praise* is equal to strength when He quoted from the Book of Psalms, saying, *"Out of the mouth of babes and nursing infants You have perfected praise"* (Matt. 21:16). The Bible's definitions of *babes* and *nursing infants* refer to those who are not yet spiritually mature enough to know how to work the Word of God. But this text demonstrates that even a newborn Christian has enough power in his praise to strengthen him and resist the devil.

When you praise the Lord, it wears the enemy out! He says, "Whew! That's too much for me. I can't take it! Stop that! Stop the praise! I'm out of here." When you magnify the Lord, the enemy loses strength and retreats.

*"O magnify the Lord with me, and let us exalt His name together"* (Ps. 34:3 KJV). You are lifting God in your words of praise and exalting His ability to change the outcome. Use part of your prayer time to praise God. Make your lifestyle one of praise and gratitude to God.

## YOUR INTERVENTION PRAYER

Father, I praise You for saving *(insert your loved one's name)*. I celebrate how You are moving in their lives to show Yourself mighty on their behalf. With joy, I look forward to seeing them in church, reading Your Word, and singing praises to Your name. I believe that great shall be the peace of *(insert your loved one's name),* and he/she is a disciple of the Lord Jesus Christ. *(Insert your loved one's name)* is like a tree planted by the rivers of living water. His/her leaves shall not wither, but whatever he/she does will prosper. *(Insert your loved one's name)* will not experience fear when the troubles of life come because he/she trusts in the Lord.

According to Ezekiel 11:19-20, I thank You that You give *(insert your loved one's name)* a devoted heart. You put a new spirit within them, taking out the hard, rebellious heart. I rejoice that You give *(insert your loved one's name)* a heart that desires to walk in Your statutes, keep Your judgments, and do them.

According to John 6:44, no one can come to Jesus unless the Father draws them. Thank You, Heavenly Father, for drawing *(insert your loved one's name)* by Your Spirit. I rejoice that You open the eyes of *(insert your loved one's name)*'s understanding and reveal the height, depth, width, and breadth of the love of God in Christ Jesus. Let the light of the gospel of Jesus Christ shine brightly in the eyes of their understanding, causing them to clearly see the salvation You have made available.

I commit to cultivating an attitude of gratitude and a lifestyle of praise. I will fill my thoughts with expectations of good and take the thoughts of fear, failure, or defeat captive. Thank You, Father, for the peace that passes all understanding that guards my heart and mind.

## BUILD YOUR FAITH

Here is a compilation of verses to help you be thankful and position yourself in praise. Spend some time developing this gratitude for the freedom and salvation of your loved one.

### ROMANS 8:37 (WET)

*But in these things, all of them, we are coming off constantly with more than the victory through the One who loved us.*

## 1 JOHN 5:4 (WET)

*Because everything that has been born of God is constantly coming off victorious over the world. And this is the victory that has come off victorious over the world, our faith.*

## 2 CORINTHIANS 2:14 (AMPC)

*But thanks be to God, Who in Christ always leads us in triumph [as trophies of Christ's victory] and through us spreads and makes evident the fragrance of the knowledge of God everywhere.*

## PSALM 68:19 (KJV)

*Blessed be the Lord, who daily loadeth us with benefits, even the God of our salvation. Selah.*

# THE APPLICATION OF JESUS' INTERCESSION

If your loved one hasn't accepted Jesus as Lord, the primary objective of the intervention is to help them see and accept Jesus' sacrifice. While they may not want to hear you preach the gospel, your prayers can set the scene for them to hear and receive. At the root of the problem is spiritual death, and the answer to that problem is to be born again. Jesus said in John 3:6-7, *"That which is born of the flesh is flesh, and that which is born of the Spirit is spirit. ...You must be born again."*

## ROMANS 5:12 (AMPC)

*Therefore, as sin came into the world through one man, and death as the result of sin, so death spread to all men, [no one being able to stop it or to escape its power] because all men sinned.*

## 1 CORINTHIANS 15:21-22

*For since by man came death, by Man also came the resurrection of the dead. For as in Adam all die, even so in Christ all shall be made alive.*

When sin entered through Adam's disobedience, spiritual death entered his heart, and Adam passed spiritual death to every person born on the earth.

It helps if we understand the difference between a *prayer of intercession* and Jesus' *work of intercession*. First, what does intercession mean? The word *intercede* means "to go between." Jesus Christ is the Intercessor and completed the *work* of intercession when He redeemed us.

### ISAIAH 59:16 (KJV)

*And he saw that there was no man, and wondered that there was no intercessor: therefore his arm brought salvation unto him; and his righteousness, it sustained him.*

First, Jesus went between mankind and Satan to disconnect us from the power that Satan had used to control us. This disconnection is described in Genesis 3:15, which says, *"And I will put enmity between you and the woman, and between your seed and her Seed; He shall bruise your head, and you shall bruise His heel."*

Then, Jesus went between God and mankind to connect us to Him with a covenant relationship. Jesus reconciled us to God!

### 2 CORINTHIANS 5:18-20

*Now all things are of God, who has reconciled us to Himself through Jesus Christ, and has given us the ministry of reconciliation, that is, that God was in Christ reconciling the world to Himself, not imputing their trespasses to them, and has committed to us the word of reconciliation. Now then, we are ambassadors for Christ, as though God were pleading through us: we implore you on Christ's behalf, be reconciled to God.*

The work of intercession is accomplished, and the benefits are made available. Jesus established the work of intercession, going between the enemy and mankind to disconnect us from his control. Also, Jesus went between God and mankind to connect us to His eternal life. The work is done!

But we have a part in the *distribution* of the intercession of Jesus. The prayer of intercession connects others to the benefits of His finished work. Our prayers are used to help our loved ones access what is already available to them.

The prayer of intercession is used to break the power of the enemy's destruction. We exercise our authority in Jesus' name and, as His representatives, take dominion over the devil, standing against his wiles, schemes, and devices. This is a major part of intervention because our loved ones who are not walking with Jesus as their Lord have no weapons to defend themselves. We are the ones who carry the weapons to stop the devil's destruction!

So, through your prayers, you "go between" your loved one and God to apply Jesus' work of intercession. Then, you "go between" your loved one and Satan by using the authority in Jesus' name to disconnect them from Satan's plan. In the same way that Jesus stopped the storm, you speak peace to the storm raging in your loved one's life. Whatever drama the devil is instigating, you can be the go-between who nullifies his destructive activity and breaks his influence.

Intercession is Jesus' job. He is the Intercessor; we are His body. Our assignment, mission, and role are His!

In English, there are words that have meanings that have changed over time. The same thing is true in the Greek language. In Greek, *intercession* originally meant "to meet face to face and converse with a person, to have an intimate and close conversation with that person." I might come to someone and say, "Sister So-and-So thinks you are offended at her. She wants you to know that she hasn't done anything to hurt you. She loves you with all her heart." I would be meeting with them and interceding face to face. I would not be standing across the room to have this discussion. Instead, it would be an intimate, close conversation.

Because of our salvation, we can come close to God and talk to Him. For example, "Father, I come to You about my son today. I pray for peace to govern his heart. Whatever situation he is facing, I ask You to provide wisdom to make the right decision." That is a face-to-face conversation with God, illustrating the original meaning of the word *intercede*.

It hasn't completely lost that aspect, but the word did take on another meaning over time. At the time of the translation of the New Testament into English, another meaning was understood. In his commentary on Hebrews 7, William Barclay said, "As it continued, the word developed to mean 'to make a petition to a king or to present a petition or a request to a king'" (*William Barclay's Daily Study Bible*).

We have the right to petition the King of kings and Lord of lords! We don't have to wait two months to get an appointment to visit Him or go through background checks and clearances. We have a right to go to our Heavenly Father anytime, day or night, and make a face-to-face petition to request help for the people we love.

## HEBREWS 7:25 (KJV)

*Wherefore he is able also to save them to the uttermost that come unto God by him, seeing he ever liveth to make intercession for them.*

143

Knowing the meaning of the word *intercede* helps us understand that Jesus is not doing our praying *for* us. Jesus is having a face-to-face conversation with God *about* us. For instance, when we come to Jesus and say, "Lord, forgive me for what I did," He is faithful and just to forgive our sins. He stands before the Father and says, "By My blood, they are forgiven. They have accessed the forgiving power of My blood. Now, I am cleansing them from all unrighteousness."

### ROMANS 8:34

*Who is he who condemns? It is Christ who died, and further-more is also risen, who is even at the right hand of God, who also makes intercession for us.*

We are ministers of Jesus' reconciliation, and His assignment on the earth is our assignment. He is at the right hand of God to be our "go-be-tween," and we are His representatives on the earth to distribute all His redemption provides.

### 2 CORINTHIANS 5:18 (KJV)

*And all things are of God, who hath reconciled us to himself by Jesus Christ, and hath given to us the ministry of reconciliation.*

As ministers of reconciliation, we connect people with Jesus, including our family members! The ministry of Jesus, His intercession, has been delegated to us so that we could "go between" to break the power of the devil and connect people to God.

## YOUR INTERVENTION PRAYER

Heavenly Father, I come to You based on what Jesus Christ accomplished when He poured out His blood and gave His life on the cross. Jesus made intercession for *(insert your loved one's name)* and completely broke Satan's hold over *(insert your loved one's name)*. I rejoice in that and apply this freedom to *(insert your loved one's name)'s* life.

According to John 3:16, I know that You greatly love and dearly prize *(insert your loved one's name)*. You love him/her so much that You sent Jesus, Your Son, to die on the cross for *(insert your loved one's name)*. Because Jesus redeemed us by His blood, *(insert your loved one's name)* can receive forgiveness of sin if he/she will call upon Jesus as Lord (Col. 1:14). Jesus Christ has paid the price to redeem *(insert your loved one's name)* with His precious blood (1 Pet. 1:19). I ask that You help *(insert your loved one's name)* see the freedom that is available in Jesus' blood.

I rejoice in Jeremiah 46:27 because You will save *(insert your loved one's name)* from the land of their exile. They will return and be quiet and at ease. Thank You, Lord, that they shall return from the enemy's land (Jer. 31:16 AMPC).

I plead the blood of Jesus over *(insert your loved one's name)* to protect them from Satan's schemes to kill or destroy them. God, I thank You for Your protection over *(insert your loved one's name)*. Guard him/her against all destruction.

# BUILD YOUR FAITH

### HEBREWS 7:25 (AMPC)

*Therefore He is able also to save to the uttermost (completely, perfectly, finally, and for all time and eternity) those who come to God through Him, since He is always living to make petition to God and intercede with Him and intervene for them.*

### 2 CORINTHIANS 1:10

*Who delivered us from so great a death, and does deliver us; in whom we trust that He will still deliver us.*

### HEBREWS 10:20

*By a new and living way which He consecrated for us, through the veil, that is, His flesh.*

### JEREMIAH 31:16 (MSG)

*But God says, "Stop your incessant weeping, hold back your tears. Collect wages from your grief work." God's Decree. "They'll be coming back home! There's hope for your children." God's Decree.*

# MARK YOUR LOVED ONE AS "OFF-LIMITS" TO SATAN

On the night before God delivered the children of Israel out of Egypt, He used the blood of the Passover lamb to mark the homes that were off-limits to the Destroyer. As a result, the people who were covered by the blood were not touched by the destruction that swept through Egypt.

## EXODUS 12:7, 13

*And they shall take some of the blood and put it on the two doorposts and on the lintel of the houses where they eat it.*

*Now the blood shall be a sign for you on the houses where you are. And when I see the blood, I will pass over you; and the plague shall not be on you to destroy you when I strike the land of Egypt.*

We live in a better covenant than these people possessed. Hebrews 8:6 says, "*But now He has obtained a more excellent ministry, inasmuch as He is also Mediator of a better covenant, which was established on better promises.*" If the people under a lesser covenant could apply animal blood and receive protection for their families, we can apply the eternal blood of the Lamb of God, Jesus Christ, and receive protection for our loved ones, also!

The phrase *"when I see the blood"* indicates that the blood was a supernatural mark visible to God that identified that person was off-limits to the destruction that was coming. The enemy cannot cross the bloodline!

On February 23, 1945, during the battle for Iwo Jima, U.S. Marines raised a flag to indicate their victory and dominion of that island. While the picture of those soldiers raising the flag is an inspiration to us, let's remember what it portrays. The flag marked that the United States had taken possession of that ground.

Take possession in Jesus' name and claim the lives of your loved ones as a territory that belongs to the Lord Jesus Christ. We aren't going to retreat or sit idly by while the enemy devours the best years of their lives. No! We are raising a banner, a blood-stained banner! You may ask, "How do I do that?"

In the Old Testament, the blood was applied to the people by Moses taking hyssop (the twigs of a wild shrub) and sprinkling the blood on them.

### HEBREWS 9:19-20

*For when Moses had spoken every precept to all the people according to the law, he took the blood of calves and goats, with water, scarlet wool, and hyssop, and sprinkled both the book itself and all the people, saying, "This is the blood of the covenant which God has commanded you."*

So, we apply the blood of Jesus over our loved ones with faith-filled words. We declare, "In the name of Jesus, I apply the blood of Jesus to cover *(insert your loved one's name),*" or "I plead the blood of Jesus over *(insert your loved one's name)* and claim them for the kingdom of God."

With every application of the blood of Jesus, we are marking our loved ones for God. Also, we are resisting the adversary and his strategies to steal, kill, and destroy. The blood of Jesus speaks! It cries out for mercy.

### HEBREWS 12:24 (AMPC)

*And to Jesus, the Mediator (Go-between, Agent) of a new covenant, and to the sprinkled blood which speaks [of mercy], a better and nobler and more gracious message than the blood of Abel [which cried out for vengeance].*

For this to be effective, we need to have faith in the blood of Jesus. So, listen to sermons and teachings and read the verses that reveal the supernatural power in Jesus' blood. As you do, your faith will grow and fill your words. Those faith-filled words provide the "hyssop" or the method of application.

## MY BLOOD IS DRINK INDEED

We have a spiritual weapon in the blood of Jesus. By faith in His blood, we connect to a covenant that will defeat the destruction in our loved ones' lives. Our faith in Jesus' blood motivates us to magnify the blood and release its power into our situation.

I want to share one of the most important activities we can engage in as we stand for intervention—communion! When we take communion over our covenant with God, at that moment, we can release our faith that the blood of God's Lamb, Jesus Christ, is covering our loved ones, protecting them from the destroyer. We can express our trust that the price of His broken body provides wholeness and restoration in the spirit, soul, and body of our loved ones.

Four times in John 6:53-56, Jesus Christ refers to His blood and the sacrifice of His body. Specifically, He refers to His body as bread and His blood as drink. Essentially, Jesus is declaring, "I am the Passover meal. I am the Lamb whose blood was applied to protect and whose body was destroyed to provide."

## JOHN 6:53-56

*Then Jesus said to them, "Most assuredly, I say to you, unless you **eat the flesh of the Son of Man** and **drink His blood**, you have no life in you. Whoever **eats My flesh** and **drinks My blood** has eternal life, and I will raise him up at the last day. For **My flesh** is food indeed, and **My blood** is drink indeed. He **who eats My flesh** and **drinks My blood** abides in Me, and I in him."*

Jesus is emphatic about the spiritual supply available in receiving what His shed blood and broken body provided. The Amplified Bible, Classic Edition says, *"For My flesh is true and genuine food, and My blood is true and genuine drink."* In Matthew 26:27-28, Jesus said, *"Drink from it, all of you. For this is My blood of the new covenant, which is shed for many for the remission of sins."* In John 6:51, He declared, *"I am the living bread which came down from heaven...and the bread that I shall give is My flesh, which I shall give for the life of the world."*

You don't have to wait until your church provides a communion service to release the life and restoration that communion provides. You can take communion in your prayer time at home and put the power of Jesus' sacrifice to work. With some juice and a piece of bread, you can open your Bible to the verses that record the words of Jesus as He celebrated Passover with His disciples and follow His example.

My favorite portion of Scripture to use when receiving communion is in 1 Corinthians 11:

## 1 CORINTHIANS 11:24-26

*And when He had given thanks, He broke it and said, "Take, eat; this is My body which is broken for you; do this in remembrance of Me." In the same manner He also took the cup after supper, saying, "This cup is the new covenant in My blood. This do, as often as you drink it, in remembrance of Me." For as often as you eat this bread and drink this cup, you proclaim the Lord's death till He comes.*

When I proclaim the Lord's death, I proclaim my victory. Jesus Christ paid for our lives to be ransomed—liberated from the destruction of darkness. As I receive the blood, I thank God for the cleansing power it makes available to my loved ones. I rejoice over the broken body as I put the cracker or bread in my mouth and say, "I worship You, Lord, for the restoration of my loved one. You desire to restore what the years of addiction have taken. You want to rebuild their lives!"

# YOUR INTERVENTION PRAYER: A COMMUNION PRAYER

Father God, I approach Your throne in Jesus' name. I come on behalf of *(insert your loved one's name)*. I claim him/her for Your kingdom as my covenant inheritance. Father, I come before You with the elements of communion to give honor to the broken body of the Lord Jesus Christ and His shed blood.

When receiving the bread:

Jesus said, "*Take, eat; this is My body which is broken for you; do this in remembrance of Me*" (1 Cor. 11:24). I honor the broken body of the Lord Jesus Christ. "*He has borne our griefs (sicknesses, weaknesses, and distresses) and carried our sorrows and pains [of punishment]*" (Isa. 53:4 AMPC). "*He was wounded for our transgressions, He was bruised for our guilt and iniquities; the chastisement [needful to obtain] peace and well-being for us was upon Him, and with the stripes [that wounded] Him we are healed and made whole*" (Isa. 53:5 AMPC). I release the power to restore every broken part of *(insert your loved one's name)* and proclaim freedom from shame to be applied to *(insert your loved one's name)*'s life.

When receiving the juice:

Jesus said, "*This cup is the new covenant in My blood. This do, as often as you drink it, in remembrance of Me*" (1 Cor. 11:25). I honor the blood of Jesus Christ that was poured out on the cross. This blood cleanses and redeems because the life of Jesus is in this blood. I apply the blood of Jesus over the mind, will, and emotions of *(insert your loved one's name)*.

Let his/her mind be free to think, choose, and feel without any demonic influence. I release the redeeming power of this blood to protect *(insert your loved one's name)* from suicidal urges and thoughts of self-harm. Let this blood send a signal that *(insert your loved one's name)* is off-limits to the destroyer. Because of this blood, no weapon formed against *(insert your loved one's name)* will prosper. Thank You for the blood of Jesus poured out on the cross to deliver *(insert your loved one's name)* from the bondage of sin. Sin doesn't have any dominion over *(insert your loved one's name)*. I believe he/she will perceive that truth and walk in it!

## BUILD YOUR FAITH

### COLOSSIANS 1:14 (KJV)

*In whom we have redemption through his blood, even the forgiveness of sins.*

### 1 PETER 1:19 (KJV)

*But with the precious blood of Christ, as of a lamb without blemish and without spot.*

## HEBREWS 9:11-14 (KJV)

*But Christ being come an high priest of good things to come, by a greater and more perfect tabernacle, not made with hands, that is to say, not of this building; neither by the blood of goats and calves, but by his own blood he entered in once into the holy place, having obtained eternal redemption for us. For if the blood of bulls and of goats, and the ashes of an heifer sprinkling the unclean, sanctifieth to the purifying of the flesh: how much more shall the blood of Christ, who through the eternal Spirit offered himself without spot to God, purge your conscience from dead works to serve the living God?*

## HEBREWS 10:19-22 (KJV)

*Having therefore, brethren, boldness to enter into the holiest by the blood of Jesus, by a new and living way, which he hath consecrated for us, through the veil, that is to say, his flesh; and having an high priest over the house of God; let us draw near with a true heart in full assurance of faith, having our hearts sprinkled from an evil conscience, and our bodies washed with pure water.*

# HOLD THE SWORD OF THE SPIRIT IN YOUR MOUTH

To be effective in battle, the sword of the Spirit must be in your mouth. If you are not saying something, you are not resisting. If you are just thinking about a Scripture, you are not actively resisting. The adversary will not leave the situation because you are thinking or hoping. You have to say something!

According to the Bible, if you have the spirit of faith, you will speak what you believe!

## 2 CORINTHIANS 4:13

*And since we have the same spirit of faith, according to what is written, "I believed and therefore I spoke," we also believe and therefore speak.*

When you pray intervention prayers, you need the Word of God infused into your conversation with God *and* in the words you say to resist the devil.

## HEBREWS 4:12

*For the word of God is living and powerful, and **sharper than any** two-edged sword.*

155

The Word of God is the sword of the Spirit. No evil or negative report can defeat you when you fight against it with the sword of the Spirit because the Word of God is the sharpest sword on the battlefield.

Where does the sword of the Spirit operate? It works in your mouth! When you are in faith, your mouth will be moving. If your mouth isn't moving, you are still in the stage where faith is being developed or established in your heart. Don't get under condemnation. Just continue in the Word until faith comes. When that happens, faith will come out of your mouth.

If you are not used to hearing yourself declare the Word of God, get used to it! Make yourself start talking out loud. Your faith is verbal. Jesus resisted the enemy, showing us the proper way to resist. He did not resist Satan's attack with mental ability or emotional strength. The Lord opened His mouth and spoke verses from the Book of Deuteronomy to whip the devil (Luke 4:1-13). Today, we have Ephesians, Colossians, 1 and 2 Corinthians, Galatians, etc. that we can use to resist the devil.

But if you are not speaking the Scripture to answer the temptations or attacks of the adversary, you are not resisting. The power of the Word is only released when you put the Scriptures in your heart and declare them with your mouth. For instance, if Jeremiah 46:27 is deposited consistently in your heart, you will have a supply of faith that the Lord will save your offspring from the land of their captivity. You will release faith in your words that they will return and be quiet and at ease. As you learn how to pray intervention prayers, you must be prepared to use the sword of the Spirit to resist the strategies of Satan.

# PRAY IT AGAIN

The Holy Spirit is your Helper in this intervention. He knows exactly what will work to help your loved one see the light and walk free of destruction. When you pray, you need His direction and insight.

## EPHESIANS 6:18 (KJV)

*Praying always with all prayer and supplication in the Spirit, and watching thereunto with all perseverance and supplication for all saints.*

In intercession, the Lord may lead you to pray some things more than once. For example, you may take authority over the mind-blinding of the enemy over and over again. It doesn't mean that your first prayer didn't work. Your loved one may have repeatedly yielded to the wrong thought or influence since the first time you prayed. The next week, the Lord may lead you to say the same thing because the enemy has attacked again. We need to follow the leading of the Holy Spirit and recognize there may be some repetition in the prayer of intercession.

I use the prayers in Ephesians 1 and 3 and Colossians 1. They are prayers inspired by the Holy Spirit. I pray them regularly and adapt them to be applied to the person I am praying for. For example, I would say, "I pray that the eyes of my child's understanding would be enlightened and fully flooded with light. That they may know what is the height, the depth, the breadth, and the width of the love of God that is in Christ Jesus. Father, I pray that You would open the eyes of their understanding. Father, I pray that they would be strengthened with might by Your Spirit in their inner man. That they would come to know what are the riches of the glory in the inheritance of the saints." Those are things you can pray over and over, and it is not a lack of faith to repeat those prayers.

# HOLDING YOUR DECLARATION OF FAITH

## MARK 5:22-23 (KJV)

*And, behold, there cometh one of the rulers of the synagogue, Jairus by name; and when he saw him, he fell at his feet, and besought him greatly, saying, My little daughter lieth at the point of death; I pray thee, come and lay thy hands on her, that she may be healed; and she shall live.*

When Jairus encountered Jesus, he made a declaration of faith that became a connection to his answer. Jairus said, "Lay Your hands on her, and she will live." Jairus' faith-filled words acted like a rope or lasso wrapped around the answer to pull it in his direction. His declaration functioned like an electrical wire that carried the current of God's healing power into his child's life. But when the situation became worse, Jairus had to cling to the statement of faith and remain connected to the promise.

If you have been standing for someone in addiction or a destructive lifestyle, you've probably already experienced moments like those Jairus faced. Maybe you received a phone call telling you your loved one is in jail. Perhaps you have just discovered what kind of drug your child is addicted to or that they have been cutting themselves or planning to commit suicide.

Whatever the report may be, we cannot allow it to change our position of faith. There is a reason that the New Testament is full of instructions to *"hold fast."* The Bible tells us to keep a firm grasp on the declaration or profession of our faith.

## HEBREWS 10:23 (KJV)

*Let us hold fast the profession of our faith without wavering; (for he is faithful that promised).*

You must hold the words of faith—the sword of the Spirit—in your mouth. Your faith-filled words maintain the connection to God's power supply, but when you begin to speak in line with the problem, you break the connection.

In Hebrews 10:23, we have a basis for our steadfast declaration—God is faithful! Because the One who promised is steadfast and trustworthy, we don't have to change what we believe or what we declare to agree. No matter what it looks like, God is faithful.

## HEBREWS 4:14 (KJV)

*Seeing then that we have a great high priest, that is passed into the heavens, Jesus the Son of God, let us hold fast our profession.*

Here is additional insight as to why we maintain our declaration of faith. We have representation at the right hand of God. Jesus is our High Priest. He receives our faith-filled words, records them as evidence of our faith, and releases His power to bring them to pass.

Jairus patiently waited while Jesus ministered to a woman who had been hopelessly ill for twelve years. During the time he waited, his little girl died (Mark 5:35). It seemed like all hope was gone.

But Jesus heard the report and immediately spoke up, saying, *"Be not afraid, only believe"* (Mark 5:36 KJV). Faith is still connected! It is not hopeless!

We do not walk by sight or base our decisions on sense knowledge evidence because it will cause us to choose defeat. Anything we could see, feel, or think is over in the temporary realm. Remember, there is a difference between things that are temporal and things that are eternal.

## 2 CORINTHIANS 4:18

*While we do not look at the things which are seen, but at the things which are not seen. For the things which are seen are temporary, but the things which are not seen are eternal.*

We have learned that *temporal* means temporary or subject to change. So, the situation is subject to change. Therefore, we cannot allow temporary conditions to determine our decisions, thoughts, or prayers.

The faith of this father rescued his daughter from death. Without the faith that Jairus brought to the table, Jesus would have been limited in what He could accomplish. Your faith is the connection!

# YOUR INTERVENTION PRAYER

Father, in Jesus' name, I choose to focus on Your Word. The temporary situation will not move me. I am strongly connected to Your promise. I have already made my faith connection for *(insert your loved one's name)*'s salvation. I refuse to fear and worry. Instead, I maintain my focus on the promise by declaring Your Word and praising You.

I pray Psalm 90:16, *"Let Your work appear to Your servants, and Your glory to their children."* Let Your work of salvation be revealed to *(insert your loved one's name)*. Draw them to Jesus Christ by Your Holy Spirit. I pray that they may obtain the salvation which is in Christ Jesus with eternal glory (2 Tim. 2:10). I ask for an outpouring of Your Holy Spirit over *(insert your loved one's name)*'s life that causes them to be saturated with Your peace, joy, and love. Let Your ways be made known to them.

I thank You, God! Your kindness will not depart from *(insert your loved one's name)* (Isa. 54:10). You are the Lord who has mercy on *(insert your loved one's name)*, and Your covenant of peace will not be removed from his/her life.

Lord, cause satanic deception to be revealed and let the truth be honored in *(insert your loved one's name)*'s life. I send the light of God's Word to *(insert your loved one's name)*'s mind to illuminate the truth of God's Word. I thank You, Father, that he/she walks in the light as You are in the light.

# BUILD YOUR FAITH

## JEREMIAH 17:7-8

*Blessed is the man who trusts in the Lord, and whose hope is the Lord. For he shall be like a tree planted by the waters, which spreads out its roots by the river, and will not fear when heat comes; but its leaf will be green, and will not be anxious in the year of drought, nor will cease from yielding fruit.*

## 2 SAMUEL 22:31-37 (AMPC)

*As for God, His way is perfect; the word of the Lord is tried. He is a Shield to all those who trust and take refuge in Him.*

*For who is God but the Lord? And who is a Rock except our God? God is my strong Fortress; He guides the blameless in His way and sets him free. He makes my feet like the hinds' [firm and able]; He sets me secure and confident upon the heights.*

*He trains my hands for war, so that my arms can bend a bow of bronze. You have also given me the shield of Your salvation; and Your condescension and gentleness have made me great. You have enlarged my steps under me, so that my feet have not slipped.*

## PSALM 18:2 (KJV)

*The Lord is my rock, and my fortress, and my deliverer; my God, my strength, in whom I will trust; my buckler, and the horn of my salvation, and my high tower.*

DAY 20

# EXPECT GOD TO WORK
# BEHIND THE SCENES

Y ou must have your mind renewed to the spiritual instructions
God provides concerning your stand of faith and prayers. Don't
consult the mind first and then check your spirit. Instead, learn
to walk by the leading of the Holy Spirit within your spirit. Walk in the
Spirit, and you will not fulfill the flesh's desires, cravings, and lusts. As
you take a defensive stand against the forces that are trying to destroy
your loved one, examine the condition of your heart.

The situation may seem desperate. You may see evidence of their
involvement in drugs or gangs. You may have noticed wounds on their
arms from injecting drugs or harming themselves. You may be watching
them drink uncontrollably. Whatever the case may be, your concern is
real. You know this can't continue!

But don't pray in panic! Your prayers need to be full of the Word—not
worry. Prayers filled with worry hinder God, while Word-filled prayers
will open the way for God to work in the life of your loved one.

Worry is an activity we cannot afford to participate in for several
reasons. First, worry is useless! Jesus explained that worry would never
change the situation.

163

## MATTHEW 6:25-27

*Therefore I say to you, do not worry about your life, what you will eat or what you will drink; nor about your body, what you will put on. Is not life more than food and the body more than clothing? Look at the birds of the air, for they neither sow nor reap nor gather into barns; yet your heavenly Father feeds them. Are you not of more value than they? Which of you by worrying can add one cubit to his stature?*

Second, worry will choke out the harvest of God's Word. Jesus made this clear in the Parable of the Sower.

## MARK 4:18-19

*Now these are the ones sown among thorns; they are the ones who hear the word, and the **cares** of this world, the deceitfulness of riches, and the desires for other things entering in **choke the word**, and it becomes unfruitful.*

Third, worry is a form of fear that will weaken your ability to believe. The dread and anticipation of the worst possible scenario are tools the enemy uses to drain your faith supply.

## LUKE 21:26 (AMPC)

*Men swooning away or expiring with fear and dread and apprehension and expectation of the things that are coming on the world.*

The believer is designed to meditate on the Word of God and build an image of hope that God's promise will come to pass. The Knox Translation says, *"What is faith? It is that which gives substance to our hopes"* (Heb. 11:1). When you have expectations produced by God's Word, faith will bring them into manifestation. But when you meditate on worry-filled thoughts, it causes dread, which is negative hope. If you expect the worst, fear gives substance to the things you dread.

Your born-again spirit will never compel you to worry. If you have a habit of worry, it is your flesh. The flesh *loves* to worry. But you are instructed to crucify the flesh! Galatians 5:24 (ESV) says, *"And those who belong to Christ Jesus have crucified the flesh with its passions and desires."*

God knows how serious the situation is in your loved one's life. He knows more than you know because He sees everything done in secret. Your job is to feed on God's promises, intercede in faith, and expect God to work behind the scenes.

## BELIEVE IN HOPE

Abraham is considered to be the "father of faith" and a "friend of God," but those are not the things about Abraham that encourage me the most. When I consider that Abraham had to stand and believe against the adversity of what he could see, it encourages me to believe.

### ROMANS 4:18 (KJV)

*Who against hope believed in hope, that he might become the father of many nations, according to that which was spoken, So shall thy seed be.*

According to this verse, Abraham believed *"according to that which was spoken."* He didn't believe what the circumstances reported. The natural evidence said it was impossible for Abraham to have a child with Sarah. They were both past the age of bearing children, and Sarah had never been able to have a child!

When you stare at a problem, it grows bigger in your perception until things begin to look hopeless. Romans 4:18 (KJV) uses the phrase *"against hope believed in hope"* to describe Abraham's struggle with his perception. His situation didn't have any hope to offer, so Abraham had to go to God for hope. He found his hope in God's words, *"So shall thy seed be."*

The Bible says that Abraham was not *"weak in faith."* Do you know what makes your faith weak? When you consider your circumstances or the circumstances surrounding your loved one, it deteriorates your faith.

### ROMANS 4:19 (KJV)

*And being not weak in faith, he considered not his own body now dead, when he was about an hundred years old, neither yet the deadness of Sarah's womb.*

Did the Bible say that his body was dead? Yes! But Abraham didn't consider that fact. Have you ever seen what your loved one is doing and said, "This is hopeless!" or "This situation is beyond repair!" If so, you know what it is like to consider the circumstances. Instead, consider the Word of God, His promises, and your covenant with God. God's Word is the truth that is settled and established in Heaven.

When people self-destruct, it affects the whole family. How do you keep from staggering when the addiction has become so bad the children are being removed from the home? How do you focus on the promise when anorexia has become so bad that all you can see are the bones sticking through your daughter's skin? How do you keep your thoughts in line with God's Word when you are on your way to the police station at 3:00 in the morning to pick up your teenager?

I am not telling you this will be a "walk in the park." But walking by faith is a better alternative to giving up and allowing the destruction to continue without resistance.

Abraham *"staggered not"* at the promise of God. Just like Abraham, you can walk in faith and become fully persuaded. Get your eyes off the problem and onto the promise. You can be strong in faith by focusing on the solution—God's Word!

## YOUR INTERVENTION PRAYER

Your Word instructs me to renew my mind, and I commit to doing it. I will cast down imaginations of loss, defeat, and failure. I will arrest any thoughts that the enemy brings to oppress me. I will purposefully insert Your thoughts and truths into my thoughts so that I see things Your way.

You said in Isaiah 55:9, *"For as the heavens are higher than the earth, so are My ways higher than your ways, and My thoughts than your thoughts."* Heavenly Father, I accept Your higher ways and thoughts. As I meditate on Your Word, build in me an inner image of Your promise. Help me develop that image into a spiritual video that can play in my imagination, showing me what *(insert your loved one's name)*'s life will be like in Your plan.

I resist the enemy in the name of Jesus and command every demonic force to stop their operations against the mind of *(insert your loved one's name)*. Lies, deception, and reasoning, I command you to be undone and removed. Let the reasonings of ungodly people be exposed to *(insert your loved one's name)* so that they see the error and the wickedness in those ideas.

## BUILD YOUR FAITH

### ISAIAH 55:7

*Let the wicked forsake his way, and the unrighteous man his thoughts; let him return to the Lord, and He will have mercy on him; and to our God, for He will abundantly pardon.*

### PSALM 22:5

*They cried to You, and were delivered; they trusted in You, and were not ashamed.*

## 1 JOHN 4:18

*There is no fear in love; but perfect love casts out fear, because fear involves torment. But he who fears has not been made perfect in love.*

## JOB 23:14 (KJV)

*For he performeth the thing that is appointed for me: and many such things are with him.*

# GOD NEVER CHANGES

We must allow God's Word to reveal His character to us because many of His traits are beyond comprehension. For instance, God doesn't change. In speaking of Himself, God said, *"For I am the Lord, I do not change"* (Mal. 3:6). Since we have never met someone who doesn't change, we must renew our minds to understand His unchangeable nature.

## JAMES 1:17 (KJV)

*Every good gift and every perfect gift is from above, and cometh down from the Father of lights, with whom is **no variableness**, neither shadow of turning.*

What does the phrase *"no variableness, neither shadow of turning"* mean? Let's compare some other translations:

- (WET) *"nor shadow which is cast by the motion of turning."*
- (VOICE) *"He is consistent. He won't change His mind or play tricks in the shadows."*
- (BBE) *"with whom there is no change."*
- (WNT) *"nor the slightest suggestion of change."*
- (GW) *"The Father doesn't change like the shifting shadows."*

When you have issues trusting people, it is generally caused by that person's lack of stability or your past experiences of trusting someone who wasn't trustworthy.

But you can't pray for your loved one if you don't completely trust God to help you. You must develop your trust in God, His Word, and His ways. Focusing on God's character holds a vital key to trusting in Him.

### PSALM 89:2 (AMPC)

*For I have said, Mercy and loving-kindness shall be built up forever; Your faithfulness will You establish in the very heavens [unchangeable and perpetual].*

By nature, God is full of mercy and loving-kindness. His faithfulness to us is unchangeable. We need to feed on verses that portray God's character until the knowledge of how He will respond is built into our hearts.

### ISAIAH 26:3-4 (KJV)

*Thou wilt keep him in perfect peace, whose mind is stayed on thee: because he trusteth in thee. Trust ye in the Lord for ever: for in the Lord Jehovah is **everlasting strength.***

In the Old Testament, the word *strength* in verse four is translated 64 times as *rock* and only five times as *strength.* The Amplified Bible, Classic Edition says, *"for the Lord God is an everlasting Rock [the Rock of Ages]."* Great benefits are available to those who know God as their Rock!

## 2 SAMUEL 22:32-33 (KJV)

*For who is God, save the Lord? and who is a rock, save our God?*
*God is my strength and power: and he maketh my way perfect.*

When you look to God as your Rock, you access His strength and power. He becomes involved in your daily decisions and develops your path.

## 1 SAMUEL 2:2 (KJV)

*There is none holy as the Lord: for there is none beside thee: neither is there any rock like our God.*

The Lord is in a rank and category all by Himself. No one compares to God's ability, strength, and might. Our Rock is set apart!

## 2 SAMUEL 22:2-3 (KJV)

*And he said, The Lord is my rock (stronghold), and my fortress, and my deliverer; the God of my rock; in him will I trust: he is my shield, and the horn of my salvation, my high tower, and my refuge, my saviour; thou savest me from violence.*

When you declare, "God is my Rock," you send a broadcast signal to alert all angels to work with you and all demons to retreat. In the same way that Psalm 91:2 declares, *"I will say of the Lord,"* you verbally authorize God to be your Rock of Ages. Put this declaration of faith in your praise. Psalm 18:46 (KJV) says, *"The Lord liveth; and blessed be my rock; and let the God of my salvation be exalted."*

Because God is unchangeable in His nature, you can rely on Him to help you reach your loved ones. His love and compassion for what they are going through are greater than the emotions you have for them. So, run to the Rock of Ages!

# YOUR INTERVENTION PRAYER

In Jesus' name, I approach Your throne of grace to receive help in this time of need. I realize that You know more about the condition of *(insert your loved one's name)* than I do. I don't need to tell You how bad things look or how I feel about this situation. I don't even need to allow those things to be in my thoughts.

So, I cast my care on You in obedience to 1 Peter 5:7. I will not worry! I will not fear! But I will build my faith in Your promise of saving my loved ones and Your willingness to rescue people in bondage. If I slip back over into worry, I ask You to show me. Help me maintain a guard over my thoughts and words. Help me to speak and think in line with the prayers I have prayed.

I ask You to show me specific things I can pray over *(insert your loved one's name)*. According to John 16:13, the Holy Spirit will guide me into truth and show me things to come. I ask You to show me the verses I can use to take a stand against the bondage in *(insert your loved one's name)*'s life. Strengthen my understanding of the authority I have in Jesus' name. Help me to know the power released when I speak Your Word. Help me to focus on Your love for me and the love You have for *(insert your loved one's name)*.

I open my heart to You. I choose to trust You for the salvation and complete freedom of *(insert your loved one's name)*. I praise You in advance for what You are going to do in *(insert your loved one's name)*'s life. Thank You for Your faithfulness!

173

# BUILD YOUR FAITH

### HEBREWS 4:16 (NLT)

*So let us come boldly to the throne of our gracious God. There we will receive his mercy, and we will find grace to help us when we need it most.*

### ISAIAH 54:13 (MSG)

*All your children will have God for their teacher—what a mentor for your children!*

### 2 PETER 3:9 (AMPC)

*The Lord does not delay and is not tardy or slow about what He promises, according to some people's conception of slowness, but He is long-suffering (extraordinarily patient) toward you, not desiring that any should perish, but that all should turn to repentance.*

### 1 PETER 5:7 (AMPC)

*Casting the whole of your care [all your anxieties, all your worries, all your concerns, once and for all] on Him, for He cares for you affectionately and cares about you watchfully.*

# WEEK FOUR

## INTERVENTION STORY:
# GOD WILL GO TO THE EXTREME

God will go the extra mile to answer our prayers of intervention, and He can be very creative too. Benjamin was released from a drug rehab and began attending church. The Lord began to restore Ben's marriage, and his wife and children moved to reunite with him. He took a job with a local landscape company and began to prosper. God was rebuilding Ben's life.

But one day, Ben relapsed and spent his entire paycheck on drugs. His wife was frantic because he had withdrawn all the money from their accounts and disappeared. He was on a binge!

When his wife called, her pastors prayed with her, asking God to intervene and speak to Ben to come home. They prayed for God to give him a wake-up call.

Ben ended up at a crack house in one of the worst parts of Kansas City, Kansas. It was an area where their church had conducted an evangelistic outreach, distributing flyers and cassette tapes with sermons from their pastor. The person who lived in the crack house had received one of the cassette tapes during an outreach months before and used the tape to record music from the radio. When they recorded over the tape, it didn't record to the end of the cassette, so when the recorded music stopped, what was left of the sermon played.

One moment, Ben was taking a hit from his crack pipe, listening to music and rocking to the beat. The next moment, the music ended, and his pastor's voice began to preach! What a "come to Jesus" moment! Ben said that he became sober in an instant. It shook him up so much that he repented on the spot and went home!

God answered that young wife's 911 call for God's intervention. Her prayer opened the door for God to reach Ben with a supernatural wake-up call. Help was sent to the scene because someone made the call that activated God's power. Every time you call, God sends the help!

# DAY 22

# HOW TO KEEP STANDING UNTIL

Is she breathing?" The 911 operator was already pulling step-by-step instructions on the computer screen to lead the caller in performing CPR.

"No! She is not breathing! I need some *help!* Please send *help!*" The hysteria began to erupt as the woman's mother realized she was the only one present to help her daughter. *How am I going to do this? I don't know CPR! I'm here by myself!*

The calm, authoritative voice snapped her back to reality. "Stay calm. The ambulance is on the way. We are going to start CPR until they arrive. I will talk you through this, but I *need* you to do this."

Holding the phone between her shoulder and head, the elderly mother followed the operator's instructions. She positioned herself above her daughter's lifeless body and placed her thin hands on the breastbone as instructed. She began the compressions with the rhythmic counting of the 911 operator's voice guiding her.

The minutes seemed to drag on with no change. Five minutes. Eight minutes. *How much longer until the ambulance arrives?* Ten minutes. Her arms and shoulders ached. Her lungs burned. Sweat mixed with her tears of frustration dripped from her face, down her daughter's cheeks as she continued the compressions.

The operator counted, "...15-16-17-18-19-20...."

"Where are they? This isn't working! I can't do this much longer!" The woman pleaded with the 911 operator.

"Ma'am. You are doing great. Help is on the way. We *must* continue until someone arrives to take over for you. Don't give up." The operator continued to direct the woman in administering the lifesaving treatment that ultimately saved her daughter's life. Looking back, she is so thankful that the voice on the other end of the phone line insisted that she continue even though it seemed hopeless.

Your loved one's intervention may not happen overnight. Will you continue standing if days turn into weeks and weeks into years? I'm not telling you to *expect* it to take forever, but be prepared to stand until it happens. Build the endurance to keep the faith flowing as long as it takes. Jesus wants you to build spiritual endurance and determination.

The Lord used an example of a widow who approached an unjust judge to request his intervention.

## LUKE 18:1 (AMPC)

*Also [Jesus] told them a parable to the **effect that they ought always to pray and not** to turn coward (faint, lose heart, and give up).*

The widow went to the unjust judge with focused determination, refusing to accept defeat. The unjust judge eventually granted her the request because he knew she would keep coming.

## LUKE 18:2-8 (AMPC)

*He said, In a certain city there was a judge who neither reverenced and feared God nor respected or considered man.*

*And there was a widow in that city who kept coming to him and saying, Protect and defend and give me justice against my adversary. And for a time he would not; but later he said to himself, Though I have neither reverence or fear for God nor respect or consideration for man, yet because this widow continues to bother me, I will defend and protect and avenge her, lest she give me intolerable annoyance and wear me out by her continual coming or at the last she come and rail on me or assault me or strangle me.*

*Then the Lord said, Listen to what the unjust judge says! And will not [our just] God defend and protect and avenge His elect (His chosen ones), who cry to Him day and night? Will He defer them and delay help on their behalf? I tell you, He will defend and protect and avenge them speedily. However, when the Son of Man comes, will He find [persistence in] faith on the earth?*

Jesus made a contrast between the unjust judge and our Heavenly Father with an emphasis on God's faithfulness to us. Jesus also declared that God would respond to our prayers quickly.

Many people take the phrase *"His chosen ones who cry to Him day and night"* to mean that we are crying out over and over about the same thing, waiting for Him to respond. That concept paints a different image than Scripture portrays.

For instance, Isaiah 59:1 (KJV) says, *"Behold, the Lord's hand is not shortened, that it cannot save; neither His ear heavy, that it cannot hear."*

Psalm 34:15 says, "*The eyes of the Lord are on the righteous, and His ears are open to their cry.*" In Psalm 34:17, the Bible reveals, "*The righteous cry out, and the Lord hears, and delivers them out of all their troubles.*" Jesus taught in John 16:24 (AMPC) that we should "*ask and keep on asking*" so that our "*joy (gladness, delight) may be full and complete.*"

We cry out to God whenever a need arises, and He continually responds to our calls. In other words, don't refrain from calling on God's help just because you asked Him for help last night. If you need help again, call on Him!

In Luke 18:8 (AMPC), Jesus asked a haunting question. "*When the Son of Man comes, will He find [persistence in] faith on the earth?*" In essence, Jesus is telling us, "If you really know My Father, His love for you, and the integrity of His covenant, you will not waver or lose heart." How can you ensure that your faith does not grow weak or waver while you wait for God to work it out? You are praying life-changing prayers, but you need to persist.

## YOUR INTERVENTION PRAYER

Father, I thank You for my position in Christ. I have received Jesus Christ as my Lord and Savior. I choose to walk in Him according to Colossians 2:6. I am rooted and built up in Him and established in the faith.

Jesus, You came to seek and save the people lost in sin. Your desire is to reach the ones who need a physician. You became sin so that *(insert your loved one's name)* could be made the righteousness of God in You. I stand in the ministry of reconciliation and release my faith for the salvation of *(insert your loved one's name)*.

I declare that no weapon turned against *(insert your loved one's name)* will succeed (Isa. 54:17 NLT). I deal with the lie of atheism and the deception of lawlessness. These weapons will not prevail in *(insert your loved one's name)*'s life. I command those chains to break and be removed from *(insert your loved one's name)*'s way of thinking.

I ask that You be a refuge for *(insert your loved one's name)* in times of trouble and hide them under the shadow of Your wings. Father, You sent Jesus to comfort the brokenhearted, to proclaim that captives will be released and prisoners will be freed (Isa. 61:1 NLT). I receive that comfort and freedom for *(insert your loved one's name)* today. I ask You to rebuild the ruins of *(insert your loved one's name)*'s life and repair the areas of his/her life that have been destroyed (Isa. 61:4 NLT).

## BUILD YOUR FAITH

### LUKE 11:10

*For everyone who asks receives, and he who seeks finds, and to him who knocks it will be opened.*

## JOHN 16:13 (AMPC)

*But when He, the Spirit of Truth (the Truth-giving Spirit) comes, He will guide you into all the Truth (the whole, full Truth). For He will not speak His own message [on His own authority]; but He will tell whatever He hears [from the Father; He will give the message that has been given to Him], and He will announce and declare to you the things that are to come [that will happen in the future].*

## EPHESIANS 3:18 (WET)

*In order that you may be able to grasp with all the saints what is the breadth and width and height and depth, and to know experientially the love of the Christ.*

## ISAIAH 49:25 (KJV)

*But thus saith the Lord, Even the captives of the mighty shall be taken away, and the prey of the terrible shall be delivered: for I will contend with him that contendeth with thee, and I will save thy children.*

# PRAY FOR THE ROOT, NOT THE FRUIT

Have you ever watched the evening newscast and prayed against the things you heard or saw in the news report? I have. It was frustrating because I was trying to pray against something that the enemy had already put in motion. As I grew in my relationship with the Lord, I learned that praying from a defensive position is not the only way to pray.

For example, a football team has a group of players who play in the offensive position and a group who play in the defensive position. The defensive players are reacting to the opponent, trying to block their plays, but the offensive players have a different focus. They are making decisions and taking actions that will score points.

We don't need to focus all our prayers on what we see the adversary doing in our loved ones' lives. At some point in our intervention praying, we turn our attention to the root and away from the rotten fruit they may be producing.

## LUKE 13:6-8

*He also spoke this parable: "A certain man had a fig tree planted in his vineyard, and he came seeking fruit on it and found none. Then he said to the keeper of his vineyard, 'Look, for three years*

*I have come seeking fruit on this fig tree and find none. Cut it down; why does it use up the ground?' But he answered and said to him, 'Sir, let it alone this year also, until I dig around it and fertilize it.'"*

In this parable, the keeper of the garden wanted time to work on the root system, indicating that the real problem is not what we see or don't see on the branches. The problem lies deeper than that. The roots need help!

The same is true as we pray for our loved ones. There are things we can pray that provide fertilizer to the ground around their root system. Some of those things are directed by the Lord and specific to their situation. Others are found in God's Word and are always beneficial regardless of the circumstance.

I remember hearing a story about a woman who came to a minister who was holding a special meeting at her church. He had been there before and was familiar with the woman's family situation. She had a teenage son who was involved with the wrong crowd and drinking and getting high every night. She nagged him about his decisions, but she couldn't control his decisions. The more she harped on him for staying out all night, the more he did it. The more she berated him about how he needed to give his life to God and quit his sinful ways, the harder he went in that direction.

She asked the minister to pray for her son, but the minister said, "I'm not going to do it!" His response shook her up. *What did he say?*

He said again, "I'm not going to pray for him because all of your negative words and worry will undo my praying."

The minister began to describe the way she lay in bed all night waiting to hear her son enter the back door. She admitted she never went to sleep until she knew he was home. Instead, she worried about him all night wondering if he was hurt or in jail. The minister said, "I know what you say about him too. You tell people how bad and unruly he is under the guise of asking them for prayer. Worse than that, you tell *him* what a bad kid he is. Your words are making it impossible for anyone's prayers to help him."

The woman was speechless. The minister was right. She did and said all of those things! She looked at him through her tears and asked, "What should I do?"

The minister softened and said, "Surround him with faith and love. Don't wait up worrying another night. Cast your care for him on the Lord and go to sleep. When you speak to him, use sweet words. Tell him you love him. Ask how he is. Have a normal conversation without emphasizing where he is missing it."

The next time the minister came to hold another meeting at the church she attended, she met him with a smile on her face. She told him the good report, saying, "I did what you told me. I began to surround him with faith and love. I stopped worrying about where he was and entrusted him to the Lord. I began to speak good things about him and to him. Before long, he noticed the change. I wasn't harping on him or berating him. One Sunday morning, he came in from being out all night. I offered him some breakfast. As we ate, he said he wanted to go to church with me that morning. I asked him if he was sure because he hadn't had any sleep, but he insisted. He gave his heart to the Lord and has been serving God ever since!" She stopped attacking the fruit of her son's ways and began to fertilize the ground around his roots!

Let's examine some things that will fertilize the soil of the heart.

# PRAYING THE ANSWER

## PHILIPPIANS 1:10 (AMPC)

*So that you may surely learn to sense what is vital, and approve and prize what is excellent and of real value [recognizing the highest and the best, and distinguishing the moral differences], and that you may be untainted and pure and unerring and blameless [so that with hearts sincere and certain and unsullied, you may approach] the day of Christ [not stumbling nor causing others to stumble].*

This verse provides an excellent fertilizer to the root system of someone who is always choosing what their flesh wants to do or yielding to the influence of the adversary. We know that God won't override a person's will, so we need our loved ones to choose Him and His ways. If they learn to value what is vital, they will choose life and light.

## PSALM 32:8 (YLT)

*I cause thee to act wisely, And direct thee in the way that thou goest.*

Turn this verse into a prayer by asking, "Lord, help *(insert your loved one's name)* to act wisely. Father, I ask that You direct them in the way they need to go." When we pray like that, we are praying for the answer instead of against the problem.

Another example of praying the answer is found in 2 Thessalonians 1:12, which says, *"That the name of our Lord Jesus Christ may be glorified in you, and you in Him, according to the grace of our God and the Lord*

*Jesus Christ."* Begin to pray that the name of Jesus will be glorified or honored by your loved one. Give His name a place of honor in their lives by declaring it over them. You can say, "I speak the name of Jesus Christ over *(insert your loved one's name)* today. Let them know the power of that name. In Jesus' name, they will see clearly. In Jesus' name, I call them into the light."

You can pull from Colossians 3:16 and say, "Let the Word of Christ dwell in *(insert your loved one's name)* richly in all wisdom" or from Ephesians 3:17, "Father, I ask that Christ may dwell in *(insert your loved one's name)*'s heart by faith and they would be rooted and grounded in love.

## COLOSSIANS 4:12

*Epaphras, who is one of you, a bondservant of Christ, greets you, always laboring fervently for you in prayers, that you may stand perfect and complete in all the will of God.*

What a great example of a prayer that digs down into the roots of someone's life and surrounds that person with a spiritual supply! We see that Epaphras prayed that they would "stand perfect and complete in all the will of God." That's what I'm talking about—Miracle-Grow!

# YOUR INTERVENTION PRAYER

I pray from Colossians 4:12 that *(insert your loved one's name)* would stand perfect and complete in all the will of God. Heavenly Father, I ask for wholeness in *(insert your loved one's name)*'s mind and emotions. I ask that You lead *(insert your loved one's name)* away from unhealthy relationships that encourage poor decisions and draw *(insert your loved one's name)* into stable, healthy relationships with people who walk in Your wisdom.

Lord, whatever lie has caused them to refuse a relationship with You, I speak to that lie to be uncovered. Father, if they blame You for something that has gone wrong or some area where they think You failed them, help them lay that blame down. Reveal Your faithfulness to them. Have mercy on their distrust and send people to witness to them about Your goodness.

I stand against all enemy forces operating against *(insert your loved one's name)* in the name of my Lord, Jesus Christ. I enforce the will of God for *(insert your loved one's name)* to be free from all oppression of the devil. Satan, I break your hold over *(insert your loved one's name)*'s thoughts. I resist your plans to destroy *(insert your loved one's name)*'s life. No weapon formed against *(insert your loved one's name)* shall be able to prosper.

God, I praise You for Your loving-kindness that is being extended to *(insert your loved one's name)*. I pray for him/her to be able to comprehend the breadth, length, depth, and height and to know the love of Christ, which passes knowledge (Eph. 3:18).

# BUILD YOUR FAITH

## ISAIAH 31:5 (AMPC)

*Like birds hovering, so will the Lord of hosts defend Jerusalem; He will protect and deliver it, He will pass over and spare and preserve it.*

## JEREMIAH 31:16-17 (AMPC)

*Thus says the Lord: Restrain your voice from weeping and your eyes from tears, for your work shall be rewarded, says the Lord; and [your children] shall return from the enemy's land. And there is hope for your future, says the Lord; your children shall come back to their own country.*

## JEREMIAH 46:27 (AMPC)

*But fear not, O My servant Jacob, and be not dismayed, O Israel. For behold, I will save you from afar, and your offspring from the land of their exile; and Jacob will return and be quiet and at ease, and none will make him afraid.*

# YOU MAY NEED A MENTAL RESET

Even though it was dark, I could see my husband's face, lit by the moonlight, relaxed and calm. He slept as if he had no concerns in the world. I wanted to be mad at him simply because he could sleep so soundly while I was tossing and turning, trying to work out the solution to the problem!

It was past midnight, and I was still trying to fall asleep. Three times, in frustration, I whispered, "Lord, I cast this care on You. I don't want to keep thinking about it. I'm going to sleep now." I turned on my side and adjusted my pillow, determined to keep the thought of my daughter's suicide attempt from drawing itself back to the forefront of my thoughts.

Every time the questions began rotating through my mind, sleep withdrew itself from me even further. *Why won't she listen to us? She is determined to rebel at anything I say.* I rehearsed her outbursts, tantrums, and demands, looking for what I could have done differently to stop the situation from escalating. I relived the argument and her threats as she grabbed her medications and ran out the door. *How could she do this again?*

I searched our apartment complex, knowing she couldn't have gone far. I found her slumped in the corner of a secluded hallway in the building next to ours. She was weeping, holding the empty bottle that was full

190

moments before. My voice shook with a strange mixture of desperation and fury as I relayed the address to the 911 operator. The ambulance rushed her to the hospital, where they pumped her stomach and admitted her to the mental health ward for observation.

In the twilight, I cleared my mind and turned my focus to the sound of my husband's breathing. It was like my mind turned itself back on. Every time I attempted to stop thinking about it, the thoughts automatically restarted. Like a train racing down the tracks, my thoughts had momentum. But they were racing in the wrong direction!

I couldn't get out of bed without waking my husband, but I needed to do something to halt this freight train of worry. I heard, "You can't fight thoughts with thoughts." I know it was the Lord leading me. Jesus dealt with wrong thoughts by speaking God's Word, *"It is written."* I knew what I needed to do.

Psalm 91 is a chapter I know by heart, so I began to whisper, *"He who dwells in the secret place of the Most High."* I continued through the entire psalm. When I finished verse 16, I started over again, continuing this process until my mind submitted to God's Word. It seemed to take at least an hour!

Before I drifted off to sleep, I repented to the Lord for allowing my mind to get out of control. The momentum of worry had been building as I spent days meditating on the problem. This caused worry to build a mental stronghold. Thankfully, God's Word is powerful enough to pull down strongholds. Since that day, I have been more diligent about keeping my mind focused on the Lord.

## ISAIAH 26:3

*You will keep him in perfect peace, whose mind is stayed on You, because he trusts in You.*

It required some discipline, but it was worth the effort. To keep my mind focused on God's promises in the middle of the drama I had to deal with daily meant that I had to examine every thought to see if it passed the test. When wrong thoughts came, I took control of them instead of the thoughts taking control of me.

# PULL DOWN, CAST DOWN, BRING IT INTO CAPTIVITY

If you are going to successfully stop the advancement of the enemy in the lives of your loved ones, you must win the mind game. The Bible assures you that you are not lacking knowledge of Satan's devices.

## 2 CORINTHIANS 2:11 (KJV)

*Lest Satan should get an advantage of us: for we are not ignorant of his **devices**.*

The word *devices* describes "the scheming of the mind." In other words, the devil uses "mind games." Since we aren't ignorant about his devices, we *can* defeat the devil's attack of doubt, fear, or sorrow. But we must recognize it to resist it.

If you allow every thought that pops into your mind, then the enemy has an open road into your life through your thoughts. He can present his lies, deceptions, and satanic suggestions, and you are willingly participating by thinking about his thoughts. Thoughts transmit images, and you will end up with the image of death and destruction by allowing Satan's words to transport his plan into your thinking.

Your faith can be hindered if your mind is clouded with thoughts of defeat. The enemy wants to convince you that your loved one will be in this situation forever. His mental game is to develop an image of failure or loss in your mind. Perhaps your mind has seen images of your child being arrested or overdosing in a dirty crack house. Maybe you have played all the "what if" scenarios in your mind. *What if she drives while drunk and dies in a car wreck? What if he gets killed by a drug dealer?*

You've got to stop that! Don't let the devil play his horror movies on the screen of your imagination. Cast down the imagination and refuse to let your mind go there. Exalt God's imaginations instead.

## 2 CORINTHIANS 10:4-5 (KJV)

*(For the weapons of our warfare are not carnal, but mighty through God to the pulling down of strong holds;) casting down imaginations, and every high thing that exalteth itself against the knowledge of God, and bringing into captivity every thought to the obedience of Christ.*

Take captive the thoughts of fear or sadness. Force your mind to think about victory. Picture your loved one with their hands raised in church, singing and praising God. You can win the mind game just like Jesus did. Open your mouth and declare what God has said, "No weapon formed against me shall prosper!"

# ARREST WRONG THOUGHTS

## 2 CORINTHIANS 10:5 (TPT)

*We capture, like prisoners of war, every thought and insist that it bow in obedience to the Anointed One.*

Every thought? Is it possible to bring every thought under control? When I first accepted Jesus as Lord, I had a lot of thoughts that were contrary to God's way of thinking. About eight years of criminal activity and drug use resulted in the mindset of a thief and junkie.

I began to learn about renewing my mind, but the enormity of the task seemed overwhelming. How would I ever get rid of the addiction thoughts I had accumulated for so long? Like a hoarder who succumbs to the layers of trash and piles of debris in their house, I felt helpless to remove the thought patterns I had spent years practicing.

Thankfully, the Lord helped me day by day. I became more aware of the thoughts I was thinking. Instead of allowing my mind to think whatever it wanted to think, I chose specific thoughts in obedience to God's instruction.

## PHILIPPIANS 4:8 (WET)

*Finally, brethren, whatever things have the character of truth, whatever things are worthy of reverence, whatever things are righteous, whatever things are pure, whatever things are lovely, whatever things are attractive, whatever excellence there is or fit object of praise, these things make the subject of careful reflection.*

194

Worry was a thought pattern that was so ingrained in my way of thinking that it took discipline to remove it. Worry seemed so natural to me that the Lord had to convince me to deal with it. When I realized how much of my mental activity was consumed with anxiety and fretting, I understood how much of my day was consumed with wrong thoughts.

As worry continues working in the mind, it gains clarity. You will sharpen the mental image of whatever you are continually thinking. Also, you will have those thoughts displayed in your actions.

## JOSHUA 1:8 (KJV)

*This book of the law shall not depart out of thy mouth; but thou shalt meditate therein day and night, that thou mayest observe to do according to all that is written therein: for then thou shalt make thy way prosperous, and then thou shalt have good success.*

As you meditate on the Word of God, you imprint your heart with the images that God's Word transmits. You can *"observe to do"* or see yourself doing *"according to all that is written therein."* That is God's method to help you walk out His will.

## PSALM 1:1-3 (KJV)

*Blessed is the man that walketh not in the counsel of the ungodly, nor standeth in the way of sinners, nor sitteth in the seat of the scornful. But his delight is in the law of the Lord; and in his law doth he meditate day and night. And he shall be like a tree planted by the rivers of water, that bringeth forth his fruit in his season; his leaf also shall not wither; and whatsoever he doeth shall prosper.*

Whatever you do will prosper because you are propelled by God's Word. But what about the words of the enemy? What happens if you meditate on the problem? If you daily rehearse the idea that your loved ones are going to be arrested, have an accident, or whatever the tormenting idea may be that bombards the mind, you will see it like a video that plays over and over.

The image will become sharper and clearer until it seems like reality. You will begin to talk and act like it is real. Then, your prayers will be hindered because you won't see "eye to eye" with God. Amos 3:3 asks us, *"Can two walk together, unless they are agreed?"* No! You have to renew the mind to agree with God's perspective so that your intervention prayers will hit the mark.

Take the thought of your loved one being saved from Acts 16:31, *"Believe on the Lord Jesus Christ, and you will be saved, you and your household,"* and meditate on it day and night. Allow an image of your loved one serving Jesus Christ and following His plan for their lives to become so sharp and clear that it seems like reality. It is based on God's Word (and God *cannot* lie)!

## YOUR INTERVENTION PRAYER

Heavenly Father, I present my mind to You for evaluation. If I have any thoughts that are contrary to Your thoughts, I ask You to show me. I want Your Word to be the way I think about everything.

I ask You to help me defeat worry, anxiety, and any form of mental fear. In 2 Timothy 1:7, Your Word says that You have given me a sound mind. According to 1 Corinthians 2:16, I have the mind of Christ. Thank You, Lord, for helping me renew my mind, as Romans 12:2 instructs.

God, I cast the burden on You in obedience to Psalm 55:22. You will sustain me. When thoughts come that try to lead me to worry, I will open my mouth, speak Your Word, and resist them. I will take those thoughts captive.

I commit to arrest wrong thoughts that come to change the image of *(insert your loved one's name)* serving You. I will purposefully think in line with Acts 16:31 and rejoice in Your truth. I take Isaiah 54:13 and apply it to my loved one, declaring, "Great is the peace of *(insert your loved one's name)* and *(insert your loved one's name)* is taught of the Lord."

Father God, in Jesus' name, I approach You for *(insert your loved one's name)*. I place my trust in You to help me know how to pray, how to witness, and how to love *(insert your loved one's name)* in spite of their bad decisions and poor choices.

The enemy wants to blind *(insert your loved one's name)*'s mind, but 2 Corinthians 4:6 declares that You command the light to shine in the darkness. God, You revealed Yourself to the apostle Paul, bringing light into his darkness. I ask You to reveal Jesus to *(insert your loved one's name)*. Show him/her Your desire to help, to rescue, to save him/her. Reveal Your goodness and mercy to *(insert your loved one's name)*. I thank You for it.

# BUILD YOUR FAITH

## PSALM 91:1-16 (AMPC)

*He who dwells in the secret place of the Most High shall remain stable and fixed under the shadow of the Almighty [Whose power no foe can withstand].*

*I will say of the Lord, He is my Refuge and my Fortress, my God; on Him I lean and rely, and in Him I [confidently] trust! For [then] He will deliver you from the snare of the fowler and from the deadly pestilence. [Then] He will cover you with His pinions, and under His wings shall you trust and find refuge; His truth and His faithfulness are a shield and a buckler.*

*You shall not be afraid of the terror of the night, nor of the arrow (the evil plots and slanders of the wicked) that flies by day, nor of the pestilence that stalks in darkness, nor of the destruction and sudden death that surprise and lay waste at noonday.*

*A thousand may fall at your side, and ten thousand at your right hand, but it shall not come near you. Only a spectator shall you be [yourself inaccessible in the secret place of the Most High] as you witness the reward of the wicked.*

*Because you have made the Lord your refuge, and the Most High your dwelling place, there shall no evil befall you, nor any plague or calamity come near your tent. For He will give His angels [especial] charge over you to accompany and defend and preserve you in all your ways [of obedience and service].*

*They shall bear you up on their hands, lest you dash your foot against a stone. You shall tread upon the lion and adder; the young lion and the serpent shall you trample underfoot.*

*Because he has set his love upon Me, therefore will I deliver him; I will set him on high, because he knows and understands My name [has a personal knowledge of My mercy, love, and kindness—trusts and relies on Me, knowing I will never forsake him, no, never].*

*He shall call upon Me, and I will answer him; I will be with him in trouble, I will deliver him and honor him. With long life will I satisfy him and show him My salvation.*

# LORD, HELP ME PRAY!

Many times, I didn't know how or what to pray about my loved one's situation. I prayed as far as I could with the knowledge I possessed. But I sensed in my heart that more was going on, and I needed to stay with it. The Bible refers to this dilemma in Romans.

## ROMANS 8:26 (AMPC)

*So too the [Holy] Spirit comes to our aid and bears us up in our weakness; for we do not know what prayer to offer nor how to offer it worthily as we ought, but the Spirit Himself goes to meet our supplication and pleads in our behalf with unspeakable yearnings and groanings too deep for utterance.*

When we don't know how to pray about a situation, we have help. The Holy Spirit comes to our aid and bears us up! This doesn't mean He will do our praying for us while we sleep. No! Instead, the Holy Spirit helps us by giving us supernatural words that are the right thing to pray in that situation. (For more understanding, see the section entitled "How You Can Be Filled with the Holy Spirit" at the end of this book.)

## ROMANS 8:26 (WET)

*And in like manner also the Spirit lends us a helping hand with reference to our weakness, for the particular thing that we*

*should pray for according to what is necessary in the nature of the case, we do not know with an absolute knowledge; but the Spirit himself comes to our rescue by interceding with unutterable groanings.*

Praying in tongues is one of the most valuable tools we can use, especially when praying for others. When there are struggles going on behind the scenes, such as thoughts of suicide or self-harm bombarding their minds, we may not be aware of it.

In many situations, we don't understand exactly what needs to happen for them to yield to God and accept Jesus, but the Holy Spirit knows! The Holy Spirit knows what they are facing and what is stopping them from receiving from God. So, we can pray from our spirits and allow the Holy Spirit to help us by giving us the spiritual utterance of what to pray. By doing this, we can pray for things that are already the will of God for their lives.

He will pray through us as we give Him utterance by speaking in other tongues.

## 1 CORINTHIANS 14:2 (AMPC)

*For **one who speaks in an [unknown] tongue speaks** not to men but **to God,** for no one understands or catches his meaning, because in the [Holy] Spirit he utters **secret truths and hidden things [not obvious to the understanding].***

While we don't comprehend, God understands the prayer in tongues. The Scripture says when we speak in tongues, we speak to God. We pray for things that are not obvious to our understanding. Yet, God hears, understands, and answers our prayers because when we pray with the help of the Holy Spirit, we are praying the perfect will of God.

201

## ROMANS 8:27 (AMPC)

*And He Who searches the hearts of men knows what is in the mind of the [Holy] Spirit [what His intent is], because the Spirit intercedes and pleads [before God] in behalf of the saints according to and* ***in harmony with God's will.***

When we intercede and don't know how to pray, He comes to meet our supplications. He comes to help us move the heavy situation. For instance, if a person's car is broken down and they need help pushing it out of the road, someone may come along to help them push it.

The Holy Spirit comes alongside to help us. In John 14:16 (KJV), Jesus Christ said, *"And I will pray the Father, and he shall give you another Comforter, that he may abide with you for ever."* The word *Comforter* is the Greek word *paraclete.* It means "one who comes alongside to help." The Holy Spirit is our Helper. When we begin praying in tongues, He comes alongside and adds His ability. If we let the Holy Spirit help us, we won't have to strain.

We have the authority to release things in the spiritual realm. But we need to develop sensitivity and an ability to hear the Lord. We *learn* to partner with Him.

When the Holy Spirit intercedes within us, He gives us the words to say. For instance, I was in an airport and saw a gate agent pick up a microphone and say, "Flight 1250 to Los Angeles will be departing. Gates will be closing in three minutes." But I couldn't hear her on the loudspeaker. Within a few moments, a recording came across the loudspeaker. It wasn't the lady's voice. She was speaking into the microphone, and it was taking her voice through a recording system. It was a voice-over that sounded like a radio announcer. That woman told the voice-over equipment what to say, and the equipment received the information and broadcast it through the airport.

The Holy Spirit gives us the words to say because we have authority on the earth. Our authority is a vocal authority, and the Lord needs us to speak some things forth. The Holy Spirit will say things so that we will declare them. Then, God has the legal access to bring them to pass. But He must use our voice!

So, the Holy Spirit picks up the receiver and tells us what to say! A spiritual language comes out. We may not understand it with our minds, but it comes from the Spirit of God Himself. It comes directly in line with His will. We can supernaturally declare things. In doing so, we supernaturally release things.

After you have prayed in the Holy Spirit, claim Mark 11:23-24 over your words. Say, "I have prayed in tongues, yielding to the Holy Spirit. I have prayed the perfect will of God. I believe I receive what I am saying. I am exercising my faith, and by faith, I receive what I have just prayed in the Spirit."

You don't have to know it to receive it. You already know it is the perfect will of God. Now, use your faith to believe and receive it.

## 1 CORINTHIANS 14:14 (KJV)

*For if I pray in an unknown tongue, my spirit prayeth....*

The Amplified Bible, Classic Edition, says: *"For if I pray in an [unknown] tongue, my spirit [by the Holy Spirit within me] prays...."*

203

## ROMANS 8:26 (AMPC)

*So too the [Holy] Spirit comes to our aid and bears us up in our weakness; for we do not know what prayer to offer nor how to offer it worthily as we ought, but the Spirit Himself goes to meet our supplication and pleads in our behalf with unspeakable yearnings and groanings too deep for utterance.*

The Wuest Expanded Translation says: *"He lends us a helping hand."* We don't always have complete knowledge of what our family members are facing and what is coming against them. But the Holy Spirit does. Once you have prayed everything you know to pray in the natural, say, "Father, I am going to take hold of this situation with the help of the Holy Spirit. I am going to pray in the Spirit and release Your will over this situation." Then, begin to pray in the Spirit.

I know we can pray in the Spirit while we do other things like folding clothes or washing dishes. But practice praying in the Spirit when you can devote time to listening and working with Him in prayer. You will gain a greater sensitivity to what He is saying.

## ROMANS 8:28 (KJV)

*And we know that all things work together for good to them that love God, to them who are the called according to his purpose.*

You may have heard this verse used to explain a tragedy. But that is not the proper context of that passage. All things work together as a response to partnering with the Lord in prayer and praying the perfect will of God by praying in the Spirit. Now that you have prayed and released faith about the situation, all things can work together for good.

Isn't that what you want? You want things to work out for good. Then, you should utilize this holy help daily and pray the will of God for that specific purpose in their lives. We are not walking in the other person's shoes or living in their world, so we will come to the end of what we know to pray. But the Holy Spirit bears us up and comes to our aid when we don't know how to pray. The Holy Spirit goes to meet our supplication and pleads on our behalf with unspeakable yearnings and groanings too deep for utterance.

## YOUR INTERVENTION PRAYER

Father God, I approach You in Jesus' name. I worship You for Your faithfulness to Your Word. I can trust in You because You are steadfast and full of integrity.

Lord, I hold fast my confession of faith for the freedom and salvation of *(insert your loved one's name)*. I act on Hebrews 10:23 and hold fast the profession of my hope without wavering because You are faithful to Your word. Because You give me victory through the Lord Jesus Christ, I am steadfast and immovable!

I will not waver or lose my courage. I will continue in faith because You love me. You love *(insert your loved one's name)* even more than I love him/her. Your desire to free *(insert your loved one's name)* and fill him/her with Your life is greater than the desire I have to see him/her free.

God, You know what *(insert your loved one's name)* needs to hear and who can reach him/her with words of truth. I pray for You to prepare the people who can speak to *(insert your loved one's name)*. Cause their paths to cross and give Your people the boldness to speak the right things to *(insert your loved one's name)*.

Lord, Your Word will not return void. It will accomplish what You please. You have sent Your Word to *(insert your loved one's name)*. I pray for every seed of truth that has ever been planted in the heart of *(insert your loved one's name)* to be watered and come forth in a harvest of revelation knowledge. The seed of Your Word is incorruptible. I praise You, Jesus, for the harvest of the Word in the heart of *(insert your loved one's name)*.

## BUILD YOUR FAITH

### 1 CORINTHIANS 15:58

*Therefore, my beloved brethren, be steadfast, immovable, always abounding in the work of the Lord, knowing that your labor is not in vain in the Lord.*

### ROMANS 8:26 (NLT)

*And the Holy Spirit helps us in our weakness. For example, we don't know what God wants us to pray for. But the Holy Spirit prays for us with groanings that cannot be expressed in words.*

## ISAIAH 49:25 (NLT)

*But the Lord says, "The captives of warriors will be released, and the plunder of tyrants will be retrieved. For I will fight those who fight you, and I will save your children."*

## ISAIAH 44:3 (AMPC)

*For I will pour water upon him who is thirsty, and floods upon the dry ground. I will pour My Spirit upon your offspring, and My blessing upon your descendants.*

# ARE YOU "WATCHING" IN PRAYER?

A significant difference between a prayer of petition and an intervention or intercessory prayer is the continued application. The Bible uses the word *watching* in the following verse to describe this application.

## EPHESIANS 6:18 (KJV)

*Praying always with all prayer and supplication in the Spirit, and **watching** thereunto with all perseverance and supplication for all saints.*

The word *watching* means "to be intent upon a thing, to exercise constant vigilance over something." It portrays how a shepherd watches over a flock. Watching in prayer requires that we be sensitive to the stirrings and promptings of the Holy Spirit. Although we won't see with natural eyes all the details or difficulties, we can pray by the prompting of the Holy Spirit and divert the danger.

# SPIRITUAL SUPPLICATIONS

Years ago, my husband and I attended a conference in another state. We left our children with safe and trustworthy adults. Our oldest was about 16 years old and stayed with one of her friends whose family attended our church. On the morning of the conference, we went for a walk outside of the hotel. My husband and I began to pray over our children and found ourselves claiming Psalm 91 over them. We went through specific verses and declared their protection. We went to church that night, and the minister preached about Psalm 91!

We had turned our cell phones off during the church service and forgotten to check them after service. But when we walked into our hotel room that evening, the phone by the bed had a flashing message light. I picked up the phone to listen to the message as my husband turned his cell phone back on. We both heard the report at the same time. "I am calling from Olathe Hospital. Your daughter was involved in an accident, and we need your permission to treat her. Please call us back."

Immediately, we called the family she was staying with to find out if she was okay. They explained that the girls had been leaving the mall when they turned into the path of an oncoming Mack truck. The car was totaled! When the ambulance pulled up to the scene, the ambulance driver remarked, "I think we will need the body bag." By the condition of the car, they couldn't imagine that anyone had lived through the wreck.

But all the girls walked away with relatively minor injuries! Praise the Lord! My daughter had an injury to her leg that required stitches and a slight concussion, but she was treated and released that night.

To God be the glory! We weren't caught off guard or unaware. The Lord prompted us to pray for protection in advance of the accident, authorizing God to supernaturally keep them safe.

## CONSTANT ATTENTION

We have another New Testament reference to watching in prayer found in Colossians:

### COLOSSIANS 4:2 (KJV)

*Continue in prayer, and watch in the same with thanksgiving.*

The Wuest Expanded Translation says, "*Be giving constant attention to prayer, constantly vigilant in it with thanksgiving.*" The Amplified Bible, Classic Edition says, "*Be earnest and unwearied and steadfast in your prayer [life], being [both] alert and intent in [your praying] with thanksgiving.*" So, we see watching and being vigilant or alert in prayer are instructions for us to follow.

### ISAIAH 21:6

*For thus has the Lord said to me: "Go, set a watchman, let him declare what he sees."*

In the Old Testament, the watchmen were positioned on the wall surrounding the city. They could see afar off from their vantage point and alert the city to the coming danger. Also, the details and insight they received from their point of view helped prepare for the next stage of battle or defense.

## 2 KINGS 9:17-18

*Now **a watchman stood** on the tower in Jezreel, and **he saw** the company of Jehu as he came, **and said,** "I see a company of men." And Joram said, "Get a horseman and send him to meet them, and let him say, 'Is it peace?'" So the horseman went to meet him, and said, "Thus says the king: 'Is it peace?'" And Jehu said, "What have you to do with peace? Turn around and follow me." So the watchman reported, saying, "The messenger went to them, but is not coming back."*

You have the advantage because you are in Christ. The Holy Spirit dwells in you and shows you things to come. You can see things in the realm of the spirit and turn situations from destruction. You can pray answers in advance of the enemy's attack that will make his weapon's useless. But you have to be alert and sensitive to the Holy Spirit.

## 1 THESSALONIANS 5:4-6 (AMPC)

*But you are not in [given up to the power of] darkness, brethren, for that day to overtake you by surprise like a thief. For you are all sons of light and sons of the day; we do not belong either to the night or to darkness.*

*Accordingly then, let us not sleep, as the rest do, but let us keep **wide awake** (alert, watchful, cautious, **and on our guard**) and let us be sober (calm, collected, and circumspect).*

You are not in the dark about things the enemy has planned. You can be led by the Holy Spirit to thwart the strategy of the devil on every hand.

# YOUR INTERVENTION PRAYER

In the name of Jesus, I pray to have a sensitivity of heart. Father, I want to learn how to recognize Your promptings and urges. I desire to be so easily persuaded by Your Spirit that You don't have to deal with me over and over. I want to learn how to respond to You immediately. Lord, teach me how to watch in prayer. Help me to be vigilant and alert in prayer.

Today, I pray over *(insert your loved one's name)*'s paths. According to Psalm 32:8, I ask You to instruct *(insert your loved one's name)* in the way he/she should go. Father, guide *(insert your loved one's name)* with Your counsel (Ps. 73:24). Lord, show *(insert your loved one's name)* Your ways and teach *(insert your loved one's name)* Your paths. Lead *(insert your loved one's name)* in Your truth and teach him/her (Ps. 25:4-5).

Heavenly Father, I speak Psalm 147:14 (GW) over *(insert your loved one's name),* that You will bring peace to his/her borders. I stand on Your Word that the seed of the righteous will be delivered, according to Proverbs 11:21.

Father, You are the God of peace who brought to life from the dead our Lord Jesus through the blood of the everlasting covenant (Heb. 13:20). In that covenant, You promised me the salvation of my family. Your Word says in Jeremiah 31:16 that my loved ones will come again from the land of the enemy. I trust You for that promise. I declare *(insert your loved one's name)* will come to the kingdom of God and leave behind the land of the enemy.

# BUILD YOUR FAITH

### PSALM 25:4-5 (AMPC)

*Show me Your ways, O Lord; teach me Your paths. Guide me in Your truth and faithfulness and teach me, for You are the God of my salvation; for You [You only and altogether] do I wait [expectantly] all the day long.*

### PSALM 32:8 (AMPC)

*I [the Lord] will instruct you and teach you in the way you should go; I will counsel you with My eye upon you.*

### PSALM 73:24 (NLT)

*You guide me with your counsel, leading me to a glorious destiny.*

### PSALM 112:4

*Unto the upright there arises light in the darkness.*

# RESPOND FROM YOUR SPIRIT

The ambulance driver was sitting in the parking lot, leisurely enjoying an afternoon cup of coffee while catching up with his partner about her family vacation, when the voice of the dispatcher broke through the silence. The words "full code" alerted the driver to flip on the blue lights as his partner entered the address of the call into the GPS.

As they rushed through the traffic with sirens blaring, they devised their plan of action, including who would take over the CPR already underway at the scene. Additional details came over the intercom, "Patient is three years of age...."

Images of his own toddler flashed into his mind, but he knew allowing the wrong emotions to enter his mind would hinder his ability to help his patient. As he grabbed the defibrillator from the back of the ambulance, he pushed those thoughts aside and turned his attention to saving the life of the little girl who lay lifeless before him.

Emotions can either be useful or detrimental to your prayers. You must know how to keep your emotions working with your prayers and not hinder them. If you allow your emotions to govern you when you pray, you will get off course because emotions are *not* safe guides. God never intended for emotions to be under the influence of the flesh. Preferably, God designed emotions to function under the leadership of your born-again spirit, where the Word of God is in charge.

When praying for someone in the grip of destruction, you never pray in panic or despair. Fear-filled prayers are dangerous. You will be more productive if you take the time to build your heart with the strength to govern your emotions and control your thoughts. In this situation, you are the spiritual "first responder" and cannot succumb to an emotional breakdown.

Ephesians 6:10 compels us to be *"strong in the Lord and in the power of His might."* To be strong in the Lord is to be spiritually strong. The prayer in Ephesians 3:16 is that they would be *"strengthened with might through His Spirit in the inner man."* So, being spiritually strong involves responding to every situation in life from the inner man instead of the flesh. Galatians 5:16 (KJV) instructs, *"This I say then, Walk in the Spirit, and ye shall not fulfil the lust of the flesh."* Again, the word *walk* refers to your daily life—the day-in and day-out responses and choices.

We put on the spiritual man by making a choice to respond from our heart, our born-again spirit.

## COLOSSIANS 3:8-10 (AMPC)

*But now put away and rid yourselves [completely] of all these things: anger, rage, bad feeling toward others, curses and slander, and foulmouthed abuse and shameful utterances from your lips! Do not lie to one another, for you have stripped off the old (unregenerate) self with its evil practices, and have clothed yourselves with the new [spiritual self], which is [ever in the process of being] renewed and remolded into [fuller and more perfect knowledge upon] knowledge after the image (the likeness) of Him Who created it.*

When you pray for your loved ones, and the anger rises because of something irresponsible they did, set it aside and respond out of your spirit. In the same way that the first responder must be professional and stay focused on what needs to be done to save the victim's life, we must stay spiritual.

## EPHESIANS 4:22-24 (KJV)

*That ye put off concerning the former conversation the old man, which is corrupt according to the deceitful lusts; and be renewed in the spirit of your mind; and that ye put on the new man, which after God is created in righteousness and true holiness.*

In this passage, the word *conversation* means behavior or lifestyle. We are responsible to *"put off"* the old behavior, the way we acted before God's love was shed abroad in our hearts. We put on the new spiritual person that we have been made in Christ.

When we train our emotions to respond to God's Word, we will be able to focus on the spiritual response that the situation requires.

## OUR POSITION IN HIM

God's Word repositions us in life. When we take our stand on God's Word and build our life on His truth, we rise to the top of the situation. We can pray for our loved ones from this position of victory. First John 5:4 says, *"For whatever is born of God overcomes the world. And this is the victory that has overcome the world—our faith."*

Faith puts us over. No matter what storm tries to push us under the water, faith causes us to float back to the top. The word *overcome* means "to subdue, conquer, overcome, prevail, and get the victory." Because you are born of God, you can subdue the attacks of the adversary and conquer doubt or fear.

Your position is vital to your victory. Jesus said in John 16:33 (AMPC), *"I have told you these things, so that in Me you may have [perfect] peace and confidence."* The key to victory is to operate from our position in Him.

Years ago, I was praying about a situation in one of my children's lives. My teenager was making decisions that placed them in danger. Continually, rules were broken, the line was crossed, and my attempts to get through to my child were useless.

I was praying as a mom with all my motherly emotions and pleas for God to change my child. One day, the Lord interrupted my prayer. He said, "You are praying from the wrong position. You are praying from your position as a mom. If you took your place in Christ, you would make more progress because the tools and weapons you need are in Christ."

From that day, I adjusted my position to pray from my place in Christ. I began to study and strengthen myself in the knowledge of who I am in Christ and the authority I have in Jesus' name.

## 2 CORINTHIANS 5:17

*Therefore, if anyone is in Christ, he is a new creation; old things have passed away; behold, all things have become new.*

When you are born again, you become new. You are made spiritually alive and equipped with righteousness, which means right standing with God. Your standing with God gives you access to His presence to get help for your loved one. You need to make your 911 call from this authorized location.

## EPHESIANS 4:24

*And that you put on the new man which was created according to God, in true righteousness and holiness.*

You can confidently approach God's throne because Jesus has made you righteous with God. In addition, you are positioned in a place of dominion so you can take authority over the devil and the forces of the curse. Jesus is seated at the right hand of God—the place of dominion and authority—and you are seated with Him!

## EPHESIANS 2:6

*And raised us up together, and made us sit together in the heavenly places in Christ Jesus.*

I once heard about a satellite that was sent into space. Although this satellite cost millions of dollars and was equipped with extensive instruments, it wasn't working properly because it wasn't in the proper orbit. For NASA to access this satellite's great potential, they had to move it into the right position. They ignited the small thrusters attached to the sides and repositioned the satellite in the correct orbit. Guess what? Everything connected!

The same is true for you. God built you with supernatural equipment and abilities, but you need to be in the right spiritual position. In the same way that the thrusters repositioned the satellite, the Word of God will move you into your place in Christ Jesus to access God's potential.

Your prayers for your loved ones are more effective when you operate in Christ. As you stand on the promises of God and strengthen your faith to receive God's help and intervention, you will see greater results.

## YOUR INTERVENTION PRAYER

Lord, I approach Your throne in Jesus' name. I ask You, according to Ephesians 3:16, to strengthen me with might by Your Spirit in my inner man. I want to stay in a place spiritually where I can pray effectively. I thank You for Christ, the Anointed One and His Anointing, who dwells in my heart by faith. I thank You that I am rooted and grounded in love.

I choose to forgive any person who has wronged me so that my faith can work effectively. I forgive *(insert your loved one's name)* for anything they have done to me. I choose to maintain my peace by refusing all worry and anxiety. As a spiritual first responder, I place the eternal salvation of *(insert your loved one's name)* as a priority over emotional turmoil or fear that would distract me. I yield to the fruit of the Spirit in my heart and allow the character of God to prevail in me. Lord, help me stay spiritually alert and focused on Your instructions.

I place *(insert your loved one's name)* into Isaiah 49:25 and declare You will contend with the one who contends with me, and You will save *(insert your loved one's name)*. According to Isaiah 54:13, *(insert your loved one's name)* shall be taught of the Lord, and great will be the peace of *(insert your loved one's name)*. By the blood of Your covenant, You have sent forth *(insert your loved one's name)* out of the pit wherein there is no water (Zech. 9:11). Thank You, Lord, for directing his/her footsteps into Your light.

I ask You, Father, in Jesus' name, to fill *(insert your loved one's name)* with the knowledge of Your will (Col. 1:9). Let *(insert your loved one's name)* know how great Your love for him/her really is. Thank You, God, for the great work You are doing in *(insert your loved one's name)*'s life.

# BUILD YOUR FAITH

## EPHESIANS 3:14-21 (WET)

*On this account I bow my knees to the Father from whom every family in heaven and on earth is named, that He would grant to you according to the wealth of His glory, with power to be strengthened through the Spirit in the inward man, that the Christ might finally settle down and feel completely at home in your hearts through your faith; in love having been firmly rooted and grounded in order that you may be able to grasp with all the saints what is the breadth and width and height and depth, and to know experientially the love of the Christ which surpasses experiential knowledge in order that you may be filled up to the measure of all the fulness of God.*

*Now to the One who is able to do beyond all things, super-abundantly beyond and over and above those things that we are asking for ourselves and considering, in the measure of*

*the power which is operative in us, to Him be the glory in the Church and in Christ Jesus into all the generations of the age of the ages. Amen.*

## ACTS 16:31 (WET)

*And they said, Put your trust at once and once for all in the Lord Jesus, and as for yourself, you shall be saved, also your household.*

# STAND IN THE GAP

## EZEKIEL 22:30

*So I sought for a man among them who would **make a wall**, and **stand in the gap** before Me on behalf of the land, that I should not destroy it; but I found no one.*

The phrase *stand in the gap* coincides with the previously stated phrase *make a wall*. The cities were protected by a surrounding wall, and they needed to defend any gap or breach in their wall. God uses this analogy in a reference that refers to intercession. He wanted someone to pray for mercy so that He would have a legal right to defer judgment, allowing the people space to repent.

Abraham, who was referred to as a friend of God (James 2:23), stood in the gap to defer the judgment that was coming on Sodom and Gomorrah.

## GENESIS 18:23-26 (AMPC)

*And Abraham came close and said, Will You destroy the righteous (those upright and in right standing with God) together with the wicked?*

*Suppose there are in the city fifty righteous; will You destroy the place and not spare it for [the sake of] the fifty righteous in it?*

*Far be it from You to do such a thing—to slay the righteous with the wicked, so that the righteous fare as do the wicked! Far be it from You! Shall not the Judge of all the earth execute judgment and do righteously?*

*And the Lord said, If I find in the city of Sodom fifty righteous (upright and in right standing with God), I will spare the whole place for their sake.*

Abraham continued asking for mercy until God agreed to spare the city if He could find ten righteous people. Although God did not locate ten righteous and judgment fell on the city, God sent angels to rescue Lot and his family. Because Abraham was willing to stand in the gap before God, his family received mercy.

God said, *"I sought* for someone to stand in the gap before Me." Even now, the Lord seeks for someone in every family, place of employment, suburb, city, state, and region who will petition for His mercy. When you stand in the broken place of your loved one's life and pray for God's love to be demonstrated, they have the opportunity to turn from their ways and walk in God's plan.

Aaron took that stand when the plague was traveling through the camp of the Israelites. The plague was judgment for something they had done, but Moses instructed Aaron to petition God's mercy by standing in the breach they had caused, holding the holy fire from the altar.

### NUMBERS 16:46-48 (AMPC)

*And Moses said to Aaron, Take a censer and put fire in it from off the altar and lay incense on it, and carry it quickly to the*

*congregation and make atonement for them. For there is wrath gone out from the Lord; the plague has begun!*

*So Aaron took the burning censer as Moses commanded, and ran into the midst of the congregation; and behold, the plague was begun among the people; and he put on the incense and made atonement for the people.*

*And **he stood between the dead and the living**, and the plague was stayed.*

Aaron's intervention allowed God's mercy to prevail. This is what happens when you pray! You are standing in the gap, making up a wall of mercy. You have a relationship with God that allows you to intervene and allow God's mercy instead of judgment!

# GIVE THE LORD NO REST

## ISAIAH 62:7 (NLT)

*Give the Lord no rest until he completes his work....*

When you are established on God's will to save your loved one, you will understand that God is not insulted by your persistence. His love is the force that is causing you to keep asking for mercy even when your loved one has repeatedly pushed the limit. The mercy of God is the source of your boldness to stand in the gap for them. God wants you to stay with your intervention praying until the job is done. Like Abraham continued the negotiations, God wants you to stay on the line, working His will into the situation with your authority.

## ISAIAH 62:7 (MSG)

*I've posted watchmen on your walls, Jerusalem. Day and night they keep at it, praying, calling out, reminding God to remember.* **They are to give him no peace until he does what he said,** *until he makes Jerusalem famous as the City of Praise.*

Paul didn't ease up on his intervention prayers when they were caught in a storm on the sea. Paul had warned them by God's revelation not to set sail, but they ignored his insight. Paul intervened for them anyway. In Acts 27:24 (AMPC), the angel said, *"God has given you all those who are sailing with you."* In verse 37 (AMPC), we discover how many people were saved by Paul's intervention prayer, *"All told there were 276 souls of us in the ship."* God granted Paul's intervention and saved 276 people, and God, who is rich in mercy, will extend mercy to your loved one in answer to your prayer!

# MAKE UP THE HEDGE

## EZEKIEL 13:5 (KJV)

*Ye have not gone up into the gaps, neither made up the hedge for the house of Israel to stand in the battle in the day of the Lord.*

The phrase *made up the hedge* is also defined as "hedged the hedge." Growing up in the hills of East Tennessee, I saw a lot of hedgerows that indicated property lines. The hedge marked where one family's property started and another's property line ended. If the hedge is missing or broken down, who can tell where the property lines are?

225

In context, the verse speaks of spiritual preparation so the nation can stand on the day of battle. If the hedge is broken, the defenses won't stand.

In our lives, who can tell where God's property line begins and ends? The enemy will trespass on your property or in the lives of your loved ones unless we mark the hedge.

God wants you to make up or rebuild the hedge. God needs a sentry on the battleground, marking the territory that belongs to God's kingdom. The salvation of our family members is promised to us.

## ACTS 16:31

*So they said, "Believe on the Lord Jesus Christ, and you will be saved, you and your household."*

God made the covenant promise to Abraham about his children. The well-being and prosperity of our families are part of our inheritance and covenant!

## GENESIS 17:7

*And I will establish My covenant between Me and you and your descendants after you in their generations, for an everlasting covenant, to be God to you and your descendants after you.*

You must claim their lives as territory for God and make up the hedge to indicate the property line. Picture this scenario. The enemy is camped in the life of your family member. He has a drug-addiction flag flying over his campsite. He has barbed wire fences of fear and shame surrounding the entire land. He has guards with armed weapons at every entry to this person's life. The guards are using addictions, pornography, or shame from their failures to hold this person in bondage. The enemy has marked their lives as his territory and claimed them as his.

You have the title deed of faith that includes the map of this territory. This property line has been torn down by sin, and the enemy has illegally claimed this property. You must take the authority of Jesus' name and reestablish the property line. Make up the hedge! Rebuild the boundary that marks this person as kingdom ground!

Every person has free will, and our prayers won't override their right to choose God or refuse Him. But our prayers supercharge the atmosphere with God's light, employ the angel armies, and open doors for God to reveal His love, compassion, and mercy to our loved ones. Our prayers resist the adversary's schemes, wiles, and strategies, tearing down things he has spent years building. Our prayers stock the shelves of their lives with spiritual answers, hope, and strength.

You can make up the hedge! God will strengthen you, but you must stand in the gap!

## YOUR INTERVENTION PRAYER

Father, in Jesus' name, I plead the blood of Jesus to cover the mind, will, and emotions of *(insert your loved one's name)*. I apply the blood of Jesus to the spirit and body of *(insert your loved one's name)*. I reclaim the territory the enemy has illegally taken. I stand up to the adversary in Jesus' name and enforce the kingdom boundary lines.

Satan, you are trespassing! I command you to leave this life. I command you to remove your weapons from *(insert your loved one's name)*'s life. In Jesus' name, I pull down the strongholds of rejection, unbelief, selfishness, and fear in *(insert your loved one's name)*'s life.

I build a wall of hope around *(insert your loved one's name)* and hedge their life with God's covenant. Let the banner of God's love be on display, marking *(insert your loved one's name)* for God.

I release angels to enforce this kingdom boundary. The devil and his forces have no power here. I declare Jesus Christ is Lord of this land. *(Insert your loved one's name)* belongs to the kingdom of God because of God's covenant with me.

Lord, I stand on Your promise and willingness to save my family. Your Word says that You will pour out Your Spirit upon my offspring and Your blessing upon my descendants (Isa. 44:3 AMPC). You will contend with him who contends with me, and You give safety to my children and ease them day by day (Isa. 49:25 AMPC).

I confess Isaiah 54:13 (AMPC) over *(insert your loved one's name)*. *(Insert your loved one's name)* shall be a disciple taught by the Lord and obedient to His will, and great shall be the peace and undisturbed composure of *(insert your loved one's name)*.

God, You know the thoughts and plans that You have for *(insert your loved one's name)*, thoughts and plans for welfare and peace and not for evil, to give *(insert your loved one's name)* hope in his/her final outcome (Jer. 29:11 AMPC).

According to Colossians 1:12-13, I give thanks to the Father, who has delivered and drawn us to Himself out of the control and dominion of darkness and has transferred us into the kingdom of the Son of His love.

I declare this into *(insert your loved one's name)*'s life. God has delivered and drawn *(insert your loved one's name)* to Himself out of the control and dominion of darkness and has transferred *(insert your loved one's name)* into the kingdom of Jesus Christ. I rejoice that Your Word will not return empty.

## BUILD YOUR FAITH

### PSALM 9:10 (AMPC)

*And they who know Your name [who have experience and acquaintance with Your mercy] will lean on and confidently put their trust in You, for You, Lord, have not forsaken those who seek (inquire of and for) You [on the authority of God's Word and the right of their necessity].*

### PSALM 13:5 (AMPC)

*But I have trusted, leaned on, and been confident in Your mercy and loving-kindness; my heart shall rejoice and be in high spirits in Your salvation.*

### ISAIAH 44:3 (AMPC)

*For I will pour water upon him who is thirsty, and floods upon the dry ground. I will pour My Spirit upon your offspring, and My blessing upon your descendants.*

# PRAYING FOR THOSE WHO SELF-HARM OR HAVE THOUGHTS OF SUICIDE

Father, I ask You in the name of Jesus to intervene in *(insert your loved one's name)*'s life. I stand in the gap for their freedom from thoughts of hurting themself or ending their life. As Your representative, I declare in Jesus' name that *(insert your loved one's name)*'s mind be free of any thoughts planted and energized by the enemy. Every demonic pressure against *(insert your loved one's name)*'s mind be broken, and every weight of oppression and depression be lifted and removed. I bind any demonic spirits that promote anger, rejection, stress, and torment as an entry point into *(insert your loved one's name)*'s life. Lord, send laborers across their path—people who can reach them with Your Word, people who will point them to You. Give those laborers boldness and bless them for ministering to my loved one.

According to Psalm 147:3, You heal the broken in heart and bind up all their wounds. I release the love of God to flood into *(insert your loved one's name)*'s heart and drive out all fear. Any tormenting mental or emotional pain be relieved in Jesus' name. Father, help *(insert your loved one's name)* forgive all who have done wrong to him/her. May that forgiveness shut the door the enemy has used to gain entrance into their thoughts.

By faith, I frame *(insert your loved one's name)*'s well-being with the following verses.

With Psalm 121:7-8, I declare, "The Lord shall preserve *(insert your loved one's name)* from all evil: He shall preserve *(insert your loved one's name)*'s soul. The Lord shall preserve *(insert your loved one's name)*'s going out and thy coming in from this time forth, and even for evermore."

With John 10:10, I declare, "Protect *(insert your loved one's name)* from all satanic stealing, killing, and destroying. Let the abundant life of Jesus Christ preserve *(insert your loved one's name)*'s heart and mind."

With Job 33:30 (AMPC), I pray, "Father, I ask You to bring back *(insert your loved one's name)*'s life from the pit of destruction, that *(insert your loved one's name)*'s may be enlightened with the light of the living."

Lord, I trust You and depend on You to help *(insert your loved one's name)*. I ask You to release Your angels to encamp around them to protect them from demonic pressure to injure themselves. Draw them to You by Your Holy Spirit, Father. In Jesus' name. Amen.

# PRAYING FOR THOSE WHO ARE DECEIVED

Father, in the name of Jesus, I thank You that You are the Way, the Truth, and the Life. You desire that *(insert your loved one's name)* has truth in his/her inward parts and that he/she walks in the freedom that comes from walking in the light of Your truth. I come into agreement with Your will and ask that You would turn *(insert your loved one's name)* from the darkness to the light and from the power of Satan to God (Acts 26:18). I stand against any deception that has been established in *(insert your loved one's name)*'s life. I bind deception and lies in the name of Jesus.

I pray for the blood of Jesus to cover *(insert your loved one's name)*'s life and break any demonic strongholds opened by witchcraft, horoscopes, psychics, or the occult. Let the light of God's truth prevail over the teaching of false religions in *(insert your loved one's name)*'s mind and over secular agendas that promote alternative lifestyles and gender confusion. Expose the lies of the enemy that have been presented to *(insert your loved one's name),* in Jesus' name.

I ask that every veil be removed from *(insert your loved one's name)*'s eyes, that he/she will not be blinded by the opinions of others, by the thoughts and ideas of the world, but *(insert your loved one's name)* will know the true voice of the Shepherd.

Lord, I ask that You bring conviction upon *(insert your loved one's name)* for any areas where they believe a lie. Show *(insert your loved one's name)* these areas and bring them to his/her mind.

Your Word says You set the captives free, and I declare today that *(insert your loved one's name)* is free of deception. I praise You and thank You that You keep *(insert your loved one's name)* safe in Your truth and that *(insert your loved one's name)* will have the desire to abide in You.

# FINAL THOUGHTS

This is not a book to be read once and set aside. It is a tool to guide you to greater effectiveness in your intervention. Start over from day one, reread the teachings, and apply the principles again. Employ the strategies and prayer directives with greater skill. When you feel weak, find your strength in God's Word and presence. Don't let the circumstances wear you down.

I want to encourage you to remain steadfast. Prayer doesn't work like a microwave or a drive-through. We are dealing with a person's will. God is patient, and His love suffers long. He will help you be patient and continue in His steadfastness. God will continue to draw your loved ones by His Spirit as you consistently give Him the legal right to deal with them.

Finally, you need prayer partners. The Bible says one can put a thousand to flight, and two can put ten thousand on the run. Our ability is multiplied when we join forces. You can submit prayer requests at www.michellesteeleministries.com or send them in a letter to our offices. I want to see you and your loved ones rejoicing with me in heaven.

# A PRAYER FOR SALVATION

Dear Heavenly Father:

I come to You in the Name of Jesus. Your Word says, *"that if you confess with your mouth the Lord Jesus and believe in your heart that God has raised Him from the dead, you will be saved."* You also said, *"For 'whoever calls on the name of the Lord shall be saved'"* (Romans 10:9,13).

I believe in my heart that Jesus Christ is the Son of God. I believe Jesus died for my sins and was raised from the dead. I am calling upon His Name, the Name of Jesus. Father, I know that You save me now.

Your Word says, *"For with the heart one believes unto righteousness, and with the mouth confession is made unto salvation"* (Romans 10:10 KJV). I do believe with my heart, and I confess Jesus now as my Lord. Therefore, I am saved! Thank You, Father.

# HOW YOU CAN BE FILLED WITH THE HOLY SPIRIT

Acts 2:38 says, *"Repent, and let every one of you be baptized in the name of Jesus Christ for the remission of sins; and you shall receive the gift of the Holy Spirit."* The Holy Spirit is given to us, the children of God, by our Heavenly Father.

Jesus told His disciples, *"But you shall receive power when the Holy Spirit has come upon you; and you shall be witnesses to Me"* (Acts 1:8). When we are baptized with the Holy Spirit, we receive supernatural power that enables us to live victoriously.

## THE HOLY SPIRIT *IN* AND *ON* THE BELIEVER

When we are born again, we receive the indwelling of the Person of the Holy Spirit. Romans 8:16 tells us, *"The Spirit Himself bears witness with our spirit that we are children of God."* When we are born again, we know it because the Spirit bears witness with our own spirit that we are a child of God; He confirms it to us. He is able to bear witness with your spirit because He lives inside of you; you are indwelt by the Spirit of God.

But Jesus speaks of another experience that follows the new birth in Acts 1:8, *"when the Holy Spirit has come upon you."* This interaction with the Spirit of God belongs to every believer.

God wants you to be full and overflowing with His Spirit. Being filled with the Spirit is like being full of water. Just because you had one drink of water doesn't mean you're full of water. At the new birth, you received the indwelling of the Spirit—a drink of water. But now God wants you to be filled to overflowing—be filled or baptized with the Holy Spirit.

## ACTS 2:1-4 (KJV)

*And when the day of Pentecost was fully come, they were all with one accord in one place. And suddenly there came a sound from heaven as of a rushing mighty wind, and it filled all the house where they were sitting. And there appeared unto them cloven tongues like as of fire, and it sat upon each of them. And they were all filled with the Holy Ghost, and began to speak with other tongues, as the Spirit gave them utterance.*

When the disciples were filled with the Holy Spirit, they began to speak with other tongues. The Holy Spirit gave them utterance, and they spoke in a language unknown to them. Today, when a believer is filled with the Holy Ghost, they will speak with other tongues too. These are not words that come from the mind of man, but they are words given by the Holy Spirit.

What is the benefit of being filled with the Holy Spirit with the evidence of speaking in other tongues? First Corinthians 14:2 reads, *"For he who speaks in a tongue does not speak to men but to God."* Speaking in other tongues is a divine way of communicating with your Heavenly Father. This is one of many great benefits.

Once you receive the baptism of the Holy Spirit, you can yield to His flow at any time, speaking in other tongues as often as you choose; you don't have to wait for God to move on you. The more you speak in other tongues, the more you will benefit from this gift. By continuing to speak in other tongues on a daily basis, you will be able to maintain a Spirit-filled life; you will live full of the Spirit.

## A PRAYER TO RECEIVE THE BAPTISM OF THE HOLY SPIRIT

Father, I see that the gift of the Holy Spirit belongs to me because I am Your child. I come to You to receive this gift. I receive the gift of the Holy Spirit by faith in the same way that I received Jesus as my Lord by faith. I believe I receive the Holy Spirit now! I believe I will speak in other tongues as the Spirit gives me utterance, just like those in Acts 2 on the Day of Pentecost. Thank You for filling me with the Holy Spirit.

As the words the Spirit of God gives you float up from your heart, you must open your mouth and speak those words out. The words will not come to your mind, but they will float up from your spirit. Speak those words out.

# ABOUT THE AUTHOR

**P**astor **Michelle Steele** knows God's life-changing power from first-hand experience. Her zeal to spread the Word stems from how Jesus miraculously delivered her from a life of destruction and addiction.

Today, Michelle and her husband, Pastor Philip Steele, co-pastor churches in De Soto, Kansas, and Little Rock, Arkansas. In addition, Michelle hosts Faith Builders, a television program provided in English and Spanish that airs on Victory Television Network and other media outlets.

The Steeles make their home in Little Rock, Arkansas, and are the parents of five children.

*Equipping Believers to Walk in the Abundant Life*
John 10:10b

**Connect with us for fresh content and news about forthcoming books from your favorite authors...**

Facebook @ HarrisonHousePublishers

Instagram @ HarrisonHousePublishing

www.harrisonhouse.com